science
short course

The Open University

S196
Planets: an introduction

An oblique view across a canyon system on Mars. The area shown is several hundred kilometres across, and the canyon is up to 10 kilometres deep in places.

The S196 Course Team

Chair and Author	David A. Rothery
Course Assessor	Steve Miller (University College London)
Critical Readers	Stuart Freake, Janet Humphreys (University of Leeds)
Course Managers	Elaine McPherson, Isla McTaggart
Science Short Course Programme Director	Elizabeth Whitelegg
Editor	Dick Sharp
Multimedia Developer	Kate Bradshaw
Graphic Designers	Jenny Nockles, Liz Yeomans
Graphic Artist	Steve Best

This publication forms part of an Open University course, S196 *Planets: an introduction*. Details of this and other Open University courses can be obtained from the Course Information and Advice Centre, PO Box 724, The Open University, Milton Keynes MK7 6ZS, United Kingdom: tel. +44 (0)1908 653231, e-mail: general-enquiries@open.ac.uk

Alternatively, you may visit the Open University website at http://www.open.ac.uk, where you can learn more about the wide range of courses and packs offered at all levels by The Open University.

To purchase a selection of Open University course materials visit the webshop at www.ouw.co.uk, or contact Open University Worldwide, Michael Young Building, Walton Hall, Milton Keynes MK7 6AA, United Kingdom, for a brochure: tel. +44 (0)1908 858785; fax +44 (0)1908 858787; e-mail: ouwenq@open.ac.uk

The Open University, Walton Hall, Milton Keynes, MK7 6AA

First published 2003. Reprinted 2004

Edited, designed and typeset by The Open University.

Printed and bound in the United Kingdom at the University Press, Cambridge.

ISBN 0 7492 5862 4

1.2

Contents

Preface

So you want to find out about planets? This is a fascinating and rapidly developing field. In this course I will introduce you to all the planets and planet-sized objects in our Solar System, and you will also discover what we know about planets orbiting stars other than our own Sun.

What attributes an object must have to merit the title of 'planet' is a matter of debate, about which you will read in Section 2.2.4. In this course we take a fairly broad, relaxed view of the definition.

The emphasis of the course is very much on what all these bodies are *like* and how they got that way. In other words, it deals with what they are made of and the processes that occur (or have occurred) on or near their surfaces. You will have the opportunity to inspect some of the amazingly detailed pictures of their surfaces and other information that has become available in recent years, thanks mainly to the space programme but also to modern telescopes. This means you will be looking at spectacular pictures of planetary surfaces, such as the one shown on the title page. If you want to track down further examples of this kind of thing I will tell you the best places to start looking on the Internet. In addition, by the time you reach the end of this course you will have picked up knowledge, experience and skills that should stand you in good stead should you decide to study other science courses.

There are some things that this course deliberately leaves out or glosses over, in order to make enough space to cover all of the above. For example, it says little about the Sun and the ways in which the Sun influences the bodies that orbit it. Nor does it delve far into practical astronomy, so you won't find an explanation of the phases of the Moon or detailed instructions on how to locate planets in the night sky. If these are the sorts of thing you want to know about, then you will find them (and more) in the companion Open University short course S194 *Introducing Astronomy*.

The various components of the present course and their functions are described in the S196 *Study Guide*. If you have not already done so, please read it and then return to this book to begin your study of the course.

1 Introduction to Chapter 1

Assuming you are now ready (i.e. you have read to the end of Section 3 of the S196 *Study Guide*), it is almost time to take a look at Chapter 1 of *Teach Yourself Planets* (*TYP*), which is called simply 'Introduction'. This is a very short chapter, but as well as setting the scene for the rest of the book it briefly reviews the history of humankind's knowledge of the planets. You will notice that the title page of this and every other chapter in the book draws attention to the main things that you will learn as you read the chapter. This can be a useful pointer to things to look out for, but there is far more in most chapters than can be adequately summarized in that way.

While you read Chapter 1, please make a deliberate effort to highlight important words or passages in the book, as suggested in Section 2.4 of the S196 *Study Guide*. You can use either a highlighter pen to ink over the key text, or an ordinary pen or pencil to underline it. Doing this will force you to decide what you think is important, and will make it easier for you to refer back to these key passages later in your study. If you are unsure how to go about this, wait until you've finished reading the chapter and have come back to this book, where you will find an Activity (Activity 1.1) that helps you to develop this aspect of active learning.

Read Chapter 1 of *TYP* now. Note that we have put a book symbol in the margin here to show you that you need *TYP* at this point. We will use it in the same way throughout this book. The symbol is easy to spot, and we are using it to try to prevent you being caught out without the right study materials to hand. Later, you will find that we show a symbol representing a CD-ROM when you need to use the S196 CD-ROM.

Return here when you have read Chapter 1.

1.1 Chapter 1 Activity

If you were at a loss as to which bits of Chapter 1 were worth highlighting, have a go at Activity 1.1 before you read the discussion of the chapter that appears in the next section. This Activity discusses which bits of *TYP* pp. 2–3 it would be helpful to highlight. Even if you think your highlighting was adequate, have a quick look at the discussion of Activity 1.1 (near the back of this book) to see if your views coincide with mine, and to note what I recommend about highlighting passages in this book too.

Activity 1.1 Highlighting key text

(*The estimated time for this Activity is 20 minutes.*)

Page 2 is the first page of standard text in *TYP*. As you might expect, much of the text on this page is of a general introductory nature. So far as I am concerned, there is nothing in the first two paragraphs that it would be terribly useful to highlight. However, the third and fourth paragraphs set out the main themes of the book. Clues that this is so come from how each of these begins: 'However, for me, the main appeal of the planets is…' and 'My main purpose in this book is…'.

With this in mind, now re-read those paragraphs and highlight (or underline) words or phrases that would help you to pick out the most important information in these two paragraphs. When you have done this, please compare what you have done with my own suggestions in the discussion of this Activity that you will find on page 109.

When you have done that, take another look at the long first paragraph of the *History of the planets* section on *TYP* p. 3. Once again, please highlight the key text, in such a way that if you return to that page in the future your eye will be immediately drawn to the important bits. My own version is illustrated in the discussion of this Activity.

It would not be feasible for me to provide examples of text-highlighting all the way through *TYP*. Instead, you will find that this book includes at least one discussion section for each chapter. These sections draw attention to key points, but they also contain additional information, additional illustrations, and discussion of what you have read in the context of this course. The first of these discussion sessions begins immediately below. Remember that you should be highlighting the key parts of this book as well as *TYP*. There is space here to jot down notes in the margin too. By way of example, I have done this for you in Section 1.2, but after that it is up to you.

1.2 Discussion of Chapter 1

Even though this is a short chapter, there are a few points worth noting. First, a distinction is made between planetary science and astronomy. Planetary science aims to understand each planet as a world in its own right, as a substantial body with recognizable processes occurring upon and within it. Astronomy, when it deals with planets at all, is more concerned with their orbital motion and their significance with respect to other bodies. Please do not form the impression that there is a gulf, or even a clear distinction, between the two disciplines. In fact there is a lot of overlap, and some would say that my definition of planetary science is too narrow. However, the book (and this course) takes pretty much a planetary science rather than an astronomical approach.

Planetary Sci deals with planets as worlds in their own rights

There is only one named section within Chapter 1, and this is entitled *History of the planets*. It points out that only five planets appear bright enough in the sky to have been known since ancient times. Until the acceptance of the theory that the Earth goes round the Sun (propounded in modern times by Nikolas Copernicus, Figure 1.1), it was not possible to realize that the Earth is itself a planet. The first of the more distant planets was not discovered until nearly 200 years after the invention of the telescope, but Galileo Galilei (Figure 1.2), a champion of the copernican theory, was very quick to use telescopes to reveal details such as landscape features on the Moon and natural satellites in orbit about Jupiter (Figure 1.3).

You will probably have gathered from the final paragraphs of Chapter 1 that I don't much care for astrology, except perhaps when treated as meaningless fun. There is absolutely no scientific basis upon which the position of the planets in our sky can influence the fate or behaviour of either individuals or groups of people on the Earth. You may be interested to know that the gravitational attraction of Jupiter when at its closest to the Earth is about ten times less than the gravitational attraction of a large bus at a distance of ten metres.

Author does not like astrology!

You will learn more about the large family of substantial icy bodies beyond Neptune (referred to on *TYP* p. 4, and of which Pluto is merely the largest known member) in Chapters 2 and 13.

Figure 1.1 Nikolas Copernicus (1473–1543), who originated the modern version of the theory that the Earth and other planets go round the Sun.

Figure 1.2 Galileo Galilei (1564–1642), who used telescopes to prove Copernicus right. This portrait was made at about the time when he made the observations shown in Figure 1.3.

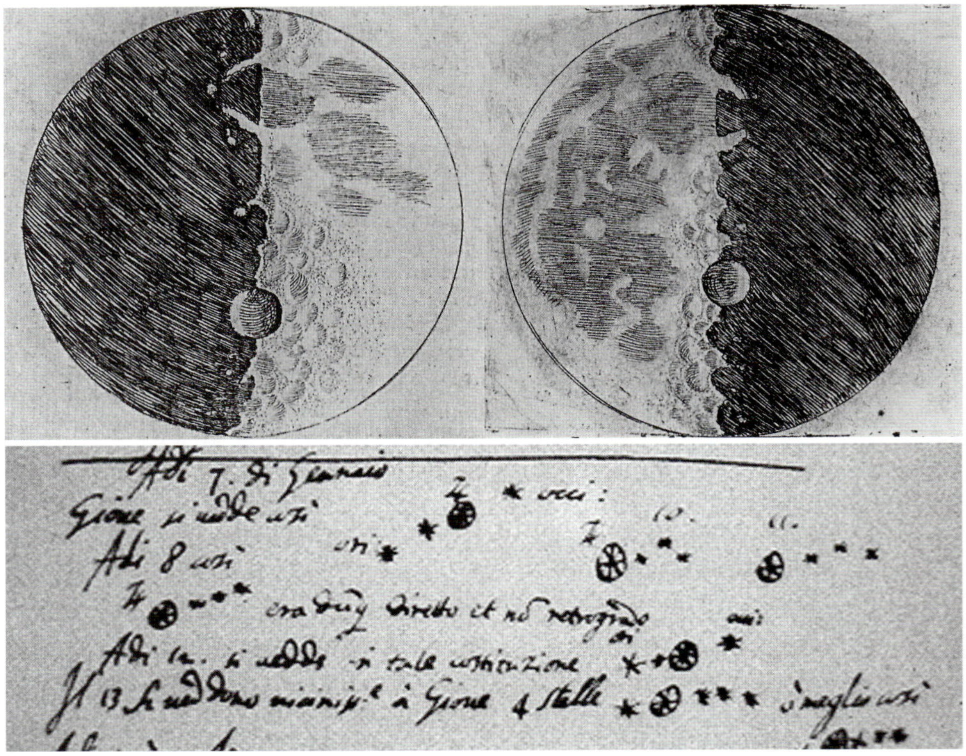

Figure 1.3 Some of Galileo's drawings, made with the aid of a primitive telescope. Above: two sketches of the Moon. Below: the changing configurations of four satellites of Jupiter, as sketched by Galileo in his (rather scrappy) notebook.

1.3 Chapter 1 optional Activities

This is not a course about *observing* the planets. However, as I say on *TYP* p. 2, there is a certain thrill associated with seeing them. You won't get a view anything like as clear as those illustrated in this course (which were obtained by visiting spacecraft or using very powerful telescopes), but even so there is nothing to compare with seeing something with your own eyes. So, when you next have the opportunity, take a look at the night sky and see if you can spot any planets. Venus, Mars, Jupiter and Saturn each appear brighter than all or most of the stars. Each of these is easily visible when it does not happen to lie too close to the Sun in the sky, but you have to be lucky or very dedicated to spot Mercury, which never strays very far from the Sun. Once a month, many newspapers print a diagram showing where to find each planet, which may be helpful if you don't know where to start. Also, the computer-based course conference (see the S196 *Study Guide*) will probably contain information about current visibility of planets. There are also various planetarium programs that you can buy to run on your PC (some are free, and there is a list at http://seds.lpl.arizona.edu/nineplanets/astrosoftware.html), but we do not expect you to go such lengths for this course. However, you won't need any help to find the Moon; if it is above the horizon, not too close to the Sun, and not hidden by clouds, you'll see it!

Therefore, I am suggesting two Activities. I realize that they may not be convenient or even possible for you to achieve, so (unlike the other Activities in this course) I am not recommending that you should do them before getting on with the next chapter. However, if you do manage one or both it ought to mean that when you later read about an object that you have seen for yourself the text will mean that much more to you.

Activity 1.2 Observing the Moon

(*The estimated time for this optional Activity is 30 minutes.*)

Try to make out features on the surface of the Moon, even if you have no optical aid available. If you have the use of a pair of binoculars you will probably be surprised by how much you can see (especially if you avoid full Moon). A telescope is even better, provided it can be held steadily enough. You will be reading about the Moon in Chapter 6, and if you can get a look at the Moon's surface before then, so much the better.

Activity 1.3 Finding planets

(*The estimated time for this optional Activity is 30 minutes.*)

Try to find at least one planet (not the Moon) in the night sky. With the unaided eye, a planet is a point of light, like a bright star. One way to tell a star from a planet, is that stars appear to twinkle because of the unsteadiness of the Earth's atmosphere. This effect becomes more noticeable towards the horizon. In contrast, planets usually appear to shine more steadily.

(a) Try to work out which planet it is. If you have never tried before, and don't have a tame astronomer by your side, this will not be easy. However, here are some clues: Venus appears very bright, and has no discernable colour. Sometimes it is too close to the Sun to see, otherwise it is either in the evening sky in the west after sunset, or in the pre-dawn sky in the east. The other three bright planets (Mars, Jupiter and Saturn) can occur at night anywhere in a belt of sky running from the eastern horizon, through a point high in the south and back down to the western horizon, but these too are sometimes too close to the Sun in the sky to be visible. (This description of where to see Mars, Jupiter and Saturn assumes you are in the northern hemisphere. If you are in the southern hemisphere the belt runs through the northern side of your sky. If you are near the equator, the belt runs overhead from east to west.) Mars has a strong red cast. When closest to Earth it appears brighter than any star. Jupiter and Saturn do not vary much in apparent brightness, and both have a slight yellowish tinge. Jupiter is the brighter of the two, and is rarely outshone by Mars.

(b) If there are any stars visible near the planet, try making a simple sketch to show their relative positions (it should be sufficient to sketch a region of sky equivalent to the span of one or both hands held at arms length). Try to find the same planet again on the next clear night, and compare its position relative to its background stars, with the aid of your sketch. Can you see that the planet has moved relative to the starry background? If so, you have identified the property that enabled the ancients to distinguish planets from the stars, as discussed on *TYP* p. 3. If your 'planet' appears not to have moved, then maybe it was just a star after all, but try again a few nights later to make sure. On the other hand, if the object moved visibly while you were watching it then it can't have been a planet either, and you were probably misled by the lights of an aircraft.

1.4 Chapter 1 questions

At the end of (and sometimes within) the discussion for each chapter, you will find a few questions (such as those below) that are intended to help you to satisfy yourself that you have understood the main points of the chapter. You will find the answers and, where appropriate, discussion of the answers at the back of this book, beginning on page 99. I strongly recommend that you attempt to answer the questions before looking at the answers, because they are good practice for your end of course assessment. However, you must not feel that it is 'cheating' if you need to refer back to information and discussion in any of the course materials to help you to answer. This course is not intended as a memory test. On the contrary, the ability to locate and extract relevant information from various sources is a skill that is valued by most scientists.

Chapter 1 is pretty basic stuff, so the questions are not very challenging. Some of the questions for later chapters are less straightforward.

Answers and comments for all the numbered questions are given at the back of the book, beginning on page 99.

Question 1.1

With which one of the following achievements is Galileo Galilei *not* associated?

A Discovering mountains on the Moon

B Being one of the first to use a telescope to observe objects in the sky

C Documenting the phases of Venus

D Discovering the planet Uranus

E Discovering four satellites of Jupiter ◀

Question 1.2

Which one of the following descriptions of an object in the sky is most likely to be the planet Venus (seen from the northern hemisphere)?

A A bright white star-like object seen high in the south at midnight

B A bright reddish star-like object seen high in the south at midnight

C A bright white star-like object seen in the east after sunset

D A bright reddish star-like object seen in the west after sunset

E A bright white star-like object seen in the west after sunset that moves perceptibly during the course of a minute

F A bright white star-like object seen in the east before dawn ◀

Introduction to Chapter 2

2

When you have read this paragraph, you should begin your study of *TYP* Chapter 2, remembering to highlight the key parts of the text as you go along. This chapter describes the nature and origin of the Solar System, and in doing so introduces you to various concepts that you will find useful when you study the planet-by-planet chapters that come afterwards. Do not worry for now if you are flummoxed by the number expressed as 6×10^{24} or reference to 'squares' and 'cubes' of numbers, because these are explained in Boxes in the discussion. Even apart from the strange numbers, you may well find this chapter more difficult than any of the others, on account of how much background material it has to provide for the later chapters to draw on. This book attempts to clarify the more daunting parts of *TYP*, so please do not be put off if you initially find it hard going. Return here when you have reached half-way down *TYP* p. 11 (i.e., before you start the section called *A short history lesson*).

2.1 Discussion of Chapter 2 pp. 6–11

There is quite a lot in this chapter, and it is worth drawing attention to several aspects, especially those that you are likely to find helpful later in the course. First though, I would like you to assess what the chapter has been about so far. Most questions in this course come at the ends of discussions, but occasionally, as here, some come earlier when I think it might be useful. Please do Question 2.1 now.

Question 2.1

The title page of the chapter includes a three-point list of things that you are supposed to learn about in this chapter. Which of those topics has been covered so far? ◀

Answering this question should have shown you that the very simple list of topics at the start of a chapter doesn't necessarily list everything in the order in which it is covered.

2.1.1 Scientific units and mathematical notation

You will note that, on *TYP* p. 7, quantities such as speed and mass are quoted in units such as kilometres per second (with kilometre abbreviated as km) and masses are quoted in kilograms (abbreviated kg). This is because scientists the world over almost always use the metric system rather than units that may be more familiar to you such as miles, feet and pounds. You won't find many non-metric units in this course.

However, planetary scientists often have to cope with such large numbers that they commonly switch to more convenient units when this makes comparisons easier. Examples you have met so far in Chapter 2 are to quote the sizes of other orbits round the Sun relative to the average distance between the Earth and the Sun, known as the astronomical unit (149.6 million km), and to quote masses of other planets relative to the Earth's mass (6×10^{24} kg).

There are two aspects to this value of the Earth's mass that are worth pointing out, in case they are concepts with which you are unfamiliar. It won't matter much in this course if you fail to come to grips with them, but they will become more important if you continue your study of science afterwards. The first is the 10^{24} part, which is an example of *scientific notation*. The second concerns the value quoted as 6, which is to do with *significant figures*. These are explained in Boxes 2.1 and 2.2, respectively.

Box 2.1 Scientific notation

You are told that the mass of the Earth is 6×10^{24} kg. *TYP* p. 22 says this means 6 million billion billion kg, which is an awful lot of kilograms! In fact, it is 6 multiplied by the number represented by one followed by 24 zeros, which is what is signalled by the 10^{24} (ten raised to the power 24). To write 6×10^{24} kg is a lot simpler than 6 000 000 000 000 000 000 000 000 kg, and you avoid the easy mistake of accidentally copying out too many or too few zeros. When you get used to the notation, 6×10^{24} kg is simpler to take in. Incidentally, you would say it as 'six times ten to the twenty four kilograms'.

The numbers expressed as 60×10^{23}, 600×10^{22} or 0.6×10^{25} are the same as 6×10^{24}. Usually it is preferable to make the number before the $\times$ take a value somewhere between one and ten (and adjust the power of ten as necessary in the second part of the number), but sometimes bigger or smaller numbers are used if it makes comparison easier.

If you need more help with powers of ten and scientific notation, you will find it in Boxes 6.1 and 6.2 of the leaflet *Background material on maths skills.*

Incidentally, when scientists these days use the term 'billion' they mean 10^9 (or 1 000 000 000, which is a thousand million) and not the old-fashioned British billion, which was a million million (10^{12}).

Box 2.2 Significant figures

You are told that the mass of the Earth is 6×10^{24} kg. What does the 6 mean? If we are to interpret this scientifically it does not mean that the mass is *exactly* 6×10^{24} kg, all it tells us is that the value is closer to 6×10^{24} than to either 5×10^{24} or 7×10^{24}. If the value had been written as 6.0×10^{24}, then we would have been justified in assuming that the true value lies closer to 6.0×10^{24} than to either 5.9×10^{24} or 6.1×10^{24}.

A value such as 6 (or six times ten to any power you like) is described as being quoted to one significant figure. A value of 6.0 (or 6.0 times ten to any power) is described as being quoted to two significant figures, and so on.

Actually, the Earth's mass has been very precisely measured, and (to four significant figures) it is 5.974×10^{24} kg. Thus, a value quoted as 6.0×10^{24} kg would be a correct representation of the true value to two significant figures, because the true value is closer to 6.0×10^{24} than to either 5.9×10^{24} or 6.1×10^{24}. However, if we wanted to quote the value correct to three significant figures, we would have to write 5.97×10^{24}, to imply that the true value is closer to 5.97×10^{24} than to either 5.96×10^{24} or 5.98×10^{24}. To quote the value as 6.00×10^{24} would imply that the true value lies closer to 6.00×10^{24} than to either 5.99×10^{24} or 6.01×10^{24}, which would be wrong, because it actually lies outside that range!

Here are a couple of questions, which test the things in Boxes 2.1 and 2.2. As with other questions, you will find the answers at the back. If the boxes left you baffled, then maybe the concepts will fall into place as you work through the answers.

Question 2.2

The distance between the Sun and the Earth is quoted in Chapter 2 as 150 million km. Write that in scientific notation, with the value in kilometres. ◀

Question 2.3

(a) Convert the answer to Question 2.2 into a value in metres (abbreviated m), given that 1 km = 1000 m.

(b) To how many significant figures is the original value quoted, and how precisely does this pin down the actual value?

(c) To four significant figures, the value of the astronomical unit is 1.496×10^8 km. How should this be written if we want to express it to just three significant figures? ◀

2.1.2 Kepler's laws of planetary motion

Apart from comparing values expressed in scientific notation, the only other kind of calculation that you will have to deal with in this course concerns Kepler's third law of planetary motion. As you are told on *TYP* p. 8, this states that the square of a planet's period of revolution round the Sun (its orbital period) is proportional to the cube of its average distance from the Sun. What *TYP* does not tell you is that it is a consequence of Kepler's other laws that a planet's average distance from the Sun is equal to half the length of the long axis of its orbital ellipse, in other words to half the straight-line distance between aphelion and perihelion in *TYP* Figure 2.1. (Figures in *TYP* and in this book use the same numbering convention. To avoid confusion as to which one I mean, when I refer to a figure simply as Figure so-and-so I mean a figure in this book. When I mean a *TYP* figure I call it *TYP* Figure so-and-so.)

Kepler's third law involves *squares and cubes* of numbers. If this concept is unfamiliar to you, refer to Box 2.3 for an explanation.

Box 2.3 Squares and cubes

When a number is multiplied by itself, the result is called the square of that number. For example if we multiply three by three we get the answer nine. Nine is said to be 'the square of three'. Or, to put it another way, 'nine is three-squared'.

We can also write this out in a more mathematical way, using numbers:

3×3 can be written more concisely as 3^2, where the superscript '2' indicates the same number multiplied by itself (so that that in the long version this number appears twice, separated by a multiplication sign).

Similarly, a number multiplied by itself twice is called the cube of that number. For example three times three times three, which works out as 27, is 'the cube of three' or 'three-cubed'.

In mathematical notation this is written $3 \times 3 \times 3 = 3^3$. Here, the superscript '3' indicates that in the long version the number appears three times, separated by multiplication signs.

Perhaps you can now see what 10^{24} means in Box 2.1. This is $10 \times 10 \times 10 \times 10 \times$, etc., with the 10 appearing 24 times.

We can also work squares and cubes backwards. For example, just as 9 is the square of 3, we can say that 3 is the 'square root' of nine, and similarly that 3 is the 'cube root' of 27.

To test whether you understand the concept of squares and cubes, please try Question 2.4

Question 2.4

You will need to use a calculator to work out at least the last two of these:

What are the values of 1^2, 1^3, 2^2, 2^3, 4^2, 4^3, 5^2, 5^3, 72^2, 72^3? ◀

It is more concise, and often more useful, to express Kepler's third law as a scientific equation than to express it in words. If we use the symbol a to represent average distance from the Sun, and P to represent orbital period, we can write

$$a^3/P^2 = k \tag{2.1}$$

using the symbol k to represent a constant value that is the same for all objects orbiting the Sun. The value of k must be constant, provided that we always measure distance and time in the same units.

To check if this works, let's try it out to compare the orbits of the Earth and Jupiter, measuring distance in AU and period in years. Inserting values of 1 year and 1 AU for the Earth into Equation 2.1 to calculate k we get the handy result:

$$k = 1^3/1^2 = 1 \tag{2.2}$$

Strictly speaking, k is not just the number 1, it also has the unit AU^3/yr^2, but we will gloss over that in this course.

If Kepler's third law works, then we ought to find that if we insert the correct values for Jupiter's average distance from the Sun and orbital period into equation (2.1), we should get the same result. According to *TYP* Table 2.1, for Jupiter a is 5.2 AU and P is 11.86 years. Let's put these values into Equation 2.1 and see what we get:

$$5.2^3/11.86^2 = 140.6/140.7 = 0.9993$$

However the value we used for Jupiter's distance was quoted only to two significant figures, which means that we can trust only the first two significant figures of this result.

- What is 0.9993 expressed to two significant figures?
- The value is closer to 1.0 than to 0.99, so the answer is 1.0.

As pointed out on *TYP* p. 8, when Kepler formulated his laws of planetary motion, these were merely precise descriptions of *how* planetary orbits work. It was not until Newton's discovery of gravity (about 70 years later) that scientists could understand *why* orbits are like this. A very brief summary of gravity is given in Box 2.4, which is all you need to be aware of for this course.

Box 2.4 Gravity

Any two objects in the Universe experience a mutual attraction by virtue of the mass that they contain. This attraction is what we call (the force of) gravity. The strength of the attraction increases in proportion to the total mass of the two bodies, and decreases in proportion to the square of the distance between the centres of the two bodies.

Thus, the more massive the bodies and the closer they are, the stronger the force. The Sun is by far the most massive object in the Solar System (its mass is 3.57×10^5 times the mass of the Earth). The gravitational attraction between the Sun and the Earth holds the Earth in its orbit round the Sun, otherwise the Earth's momentum would allow it to fly off into distant space. The size and period of any planet's orbit plus a knowledge of the laws of gravity enable the mass of the star (or, strictly, the combined mass of the star and the planet) to be calculated. When a planet has a relatively small satellite, measurements of the satellite's orbit about the planet allow the mass of the planet to be calculated using the same principles.

2.1.3 Planetary orbits and planetary spin

TYP Figure 2.2 is a scale drawing of the Solar System, seen as if looking at it at right angles to the ecliptic. You may have noticed that the orbits of Venus and Mercury are too small to include, but this drawing has the advantage of showing the true shapes of those orbits that can be shown. In contrast, Figure 2.1a has been drawn in such a way as to include the orbits of all the planets, so you may find this more useful. However, this is an oblique view, which makes the orbits appear far more elliptical than they truly are. The planets, and even the Sun itself, are too small to show at their correct relative sizes on a scale diagram of their orbits, but their sizes are compared correctly in Figure 2.1b.

A common cause of confusion among students lies in the distinction between the meanings of 'rotation' and 'revolution' as applied to a planet, so I want to try to make this completely clear to you. Rotation refers to a planet spinning on its axis. For example, the Earth's spin is what produces the alternation between day and night. The time that it takes a planet to spin once is described as its 'rotation period'. One rotation of the Earth gives us the unit of time that we call a day. Different planets spin at different rates, and so their own day-length is different from that of the Earth.

The word 'revolution' refers to a planet travelling round the Sun. When it has completed one revolution it has travelled all the way round its orbit. The length of time taken to do this is described as the planet's orbital period.

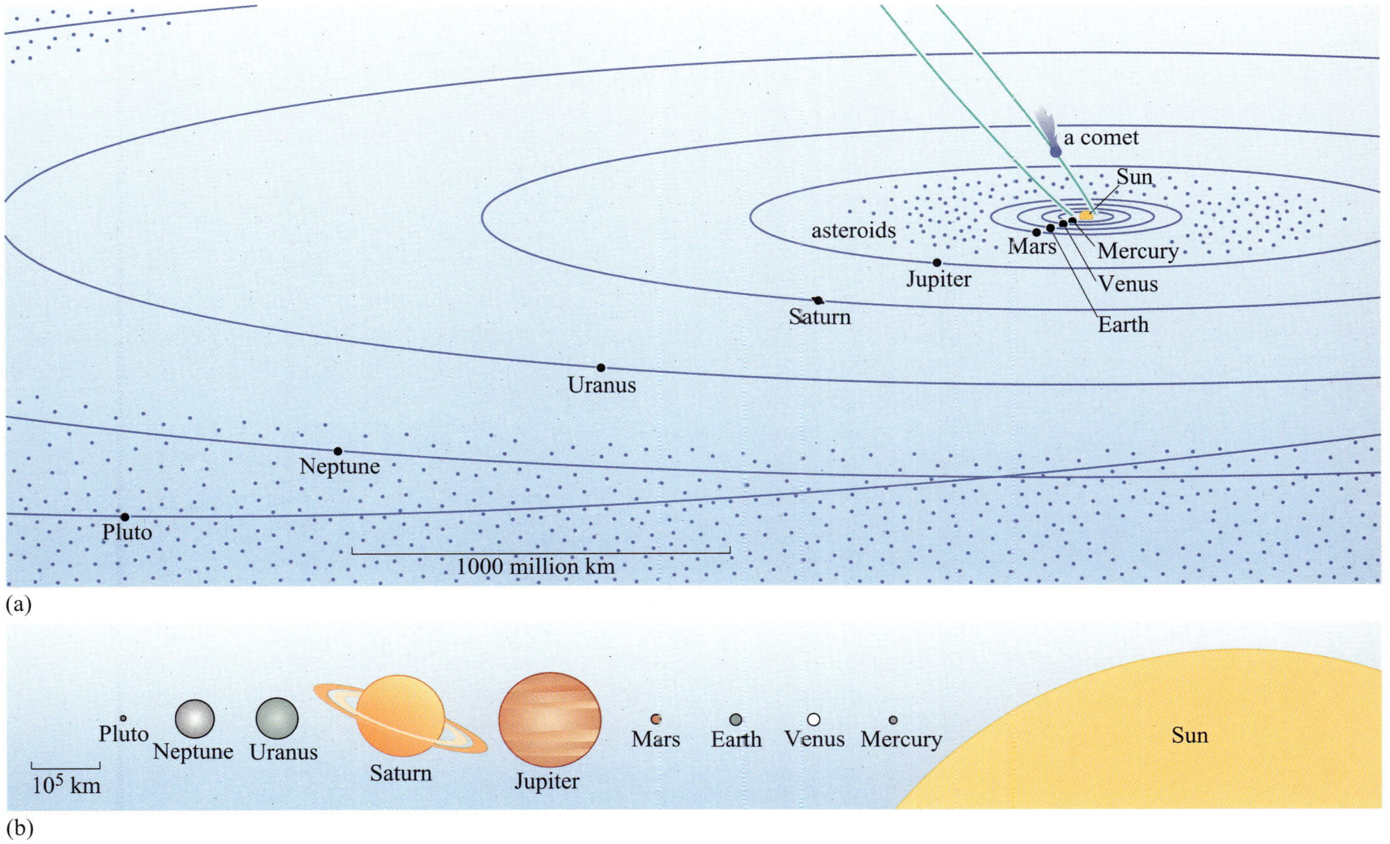

Figure 2.1 (a) Diagrammatic summary of the Solar System, as seen from an oblique viewpoint. Refer to *TYP* Figure 2.2 for the true shapes of the orbits. (b) The relative sizes of the planets and the Sun.

This section of *TYP* also refers to the direction in which a planet's axis of rotation points. For all the planets in our Solar System, this direction changes only very slowly, and can be regarded as fixed when considering a single orbit. Figure 2.2 shows how, when a planet's axis of rotation is inclined (in other words, is not perpendicular to the plane of its orbit), the solar illumination of the planet changes as it progresses round its orbit, which is what causes the seasons.

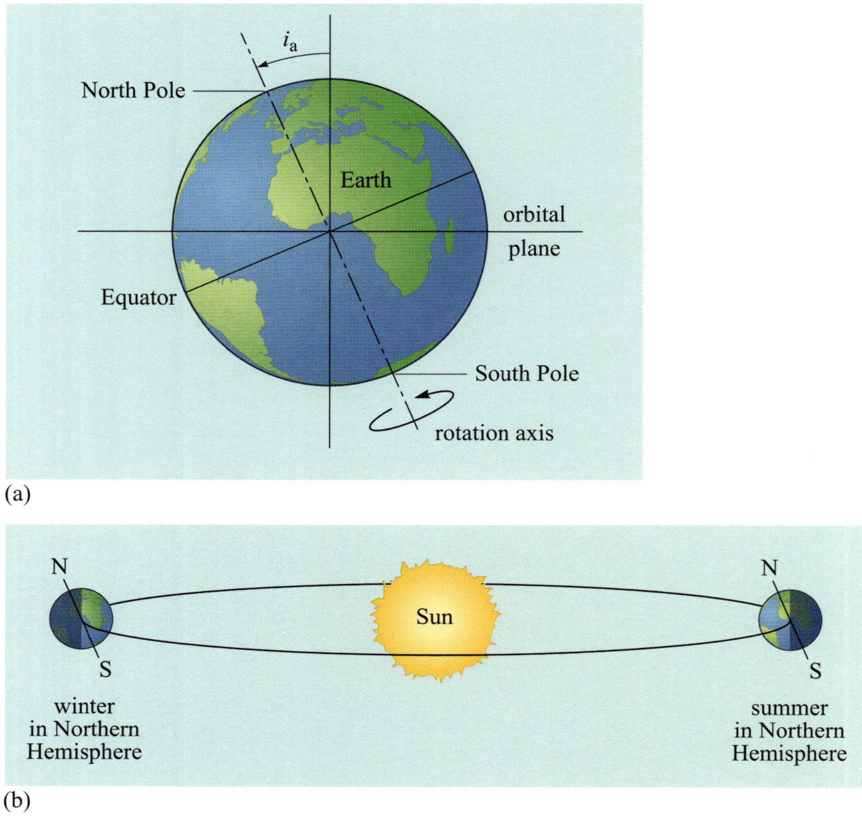

Figure 2.2 (a) The axial inclination, i_a, of a planet (in this case the Earth), which is the amount by which its axis of rotation is tilted relative to its orbit. (b) Alternating seasons as a planet with an inclined axis orbits the Sun.

There is a slight complication in the relationship between a planet's day-length and its rotation period, because the direction towards the Sun from a planet's centre is continuously changing because of the planet's progress round its orbit. Because of this, rotation of a planet is measured not relative to the Sun but relative to objects beyond the Solar System whose positions can be regarded as unchanging over the time-scale concerned. This results in a difference between rotation period and day-length, which is very slight for a rapidly rotating planet (such as the Earth) but can be very large for a slowly rotating planet. Do not worry about this for now. You will have a chance to come to grips with this tricky concept in Chapter 3.

Now complete your study of *TYP* Chapter 2, and return here when you have reached the end.

2.2 Discussion of Chapter 2 pp. 11–23

I am not going to discuss every headed section in this part of the chapter. Rather, I will attempt to clarify some of the rather complex matters introduced in this part of *TYP* and also discuss some related topics that are not developed in *TYP* but which are relevant to this course.

2.2.1 Origin of the Solar System

From the section entitled *A short history lesson* (p. 11) onwards, Chapter 2 is mostly concerned with describing the manner in which, according to most planetary scientists, the Solar System came into being and how it subsequently evolved to result in the planets and other bodies that we see today. It is worth pointing out that although the essence of that story is fairly well accepted, there is still lively debate about many of the details. For example, in the first edition of *TYP* (published in 2000) I quoted a time of 100 million years to build an Earth-sized planet. However, new research results announced in 2002 led me to halve this estimate to 50 million years for the second edition (published in 2003), which is the one you have.

Many people find it hard to visualize some of the events in the Solar System's early history, so I am providing some artist's impressions to show what things might have looked like, as Figures 2.3–2.6.

Figure 2.3 The solar nebula, as it might have looked while planetesimals were growing within it.

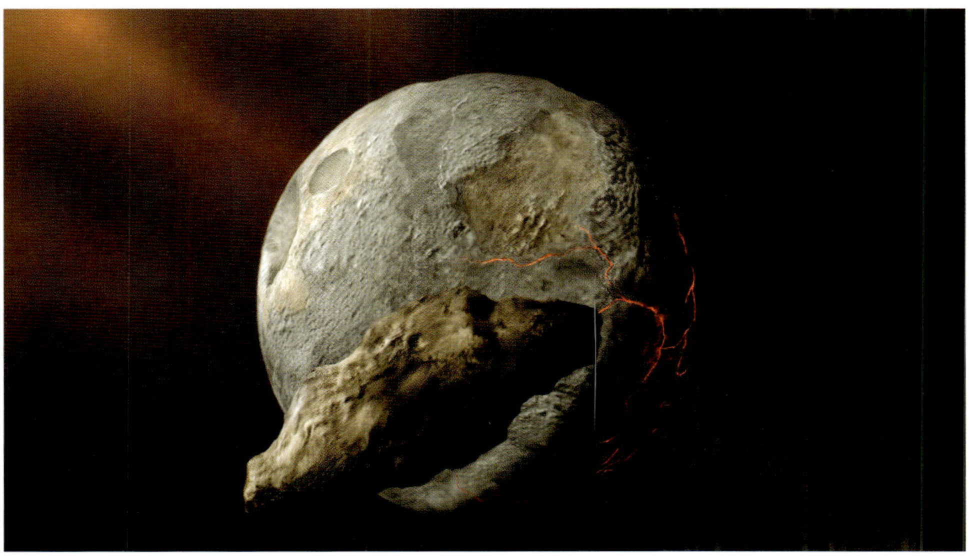

Figure 2.4 A planetary embryo, whose growth has outpaced that of all other planetesimals in the neighbourhood (such as the small irregular body visible in the foreground). This body is sufficiently large for its own gravity to pull it into a spherical shape. Its interior may or may not be sufficiently hot to allow differentiation to take place. However, this process will certainly begin as soon as this body is involved in a 'giant impact' collision with another planetary embryo of comparable size.

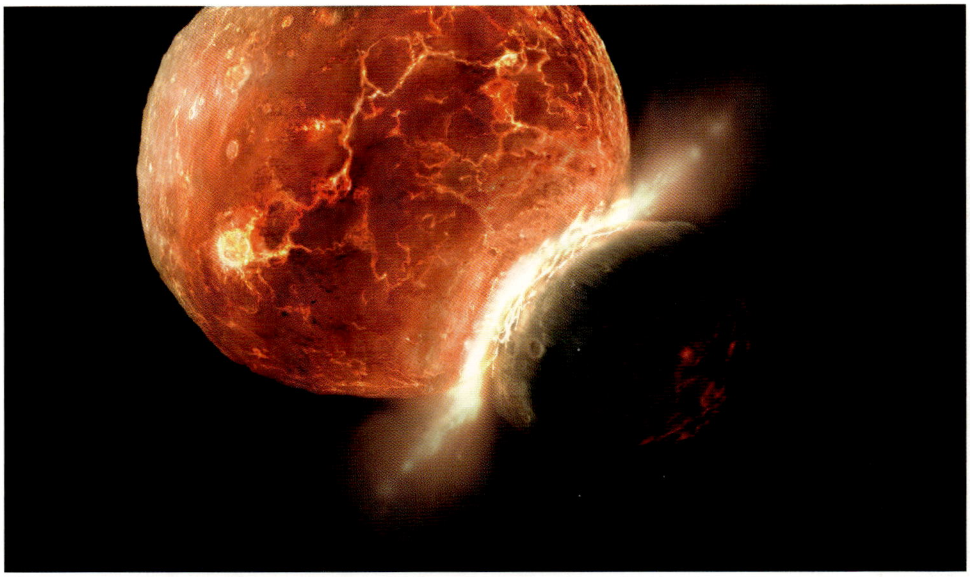

Figure 2.5 A giant impact collision between two planetary embryos. The result is usually a single body (which is still described as a planetary embryo) containing most of the mass of the two planetary embryos that collided to form it. Heat generated by the collision melts much of the body, allowing its interior to differentiate.

Figure 2.6 A young terrestrial planet (background) that has just been struck by a large asteroid or comet. Another projectile that may hit the planet is visible in the foreground. Impacts such as these were relatively common until about 3.9 billion years ago, but still occur occasionally today.

2.2.2 Impact craters

TYP Figure 2.4 illustrates the formation of an impact crater in cross-section, but does not give a very good impression of what an impact crater looks like. *TYP* has plenty of pictures of impact craters in later chapters, but to save you hunting for those, Figure 2.7 shows you what impact craters look like.

Many people have trouble visualizing the topography in pictures of planetary surfaces. Sometimes, what is really a hill appears to be a hole (and vice versa) and what is really a ridge appears to be a valley (and vice versa). Box 2.5 tries to help you overcome this optical illusion.

Figure 2.7 Impact craters on the Moon, photographed obliquely from the Apollo 11 spacecraft in lunar orbit. Sunlight is coming from the upper right. The largest crater is 80 km across, and is the only one here with an obvious central peak (in fact it has a group of central peaks). This crater also has clearly visible terracing on its inward-facing wall, and you should also be able to satisfy yourself that the floor of the crater is lower than the terrain beyond the rim. The smallest craters visible in the foreground are about 100 m across. (The same area is shown from a slightly different perspective in *TYP* Figure 6.4.)

Box 2.5 Seeing topography the right-way round in pictures of planetary surfaces

When you look at a picture of a planetary surface, shadows give the best clues as to the topography. If the caption tells you from which way the illumination is coming you should be able to distinguish between hills and holes by working out where the shadow should be in each case. Figure 2.8 is an enlargement of part of Figure 2.7, with labels to indicate some of the topographic clues. For example, the labelled peaks near the centre of the large crater cast shadows on their lower left sides. You are told that the sunlight is coming from the upper right, so these have to be hills rather than holes.

The craters in Figures 2.7 and 2.8 appear elliptical merely because the view is oblique. Vertical views show these craters to be circular.

Look carefully at the feature near the central peaks labelled X in Figure 2.8. Part of this is bright (sunlit) and the other part of it is dark (in shadow). Bearing in mind which way the sunlight is coming from, try to deduce whether this is a hill or a hole.

This feature is brightly lit on its left side and shadowed on its right side. As the sunlight is coming from the right and yet it is the right side that is shadowed, this feature cannot be a hill like the nearby central peaks. On the contrary, it must be a hole. In fact it is a small crater, which must have been formed by a smaller impact at an unknown time after the large crater was formed.

If when you look at this picture you perceive the topography the right way round, then that's fine. However, if you see it 'inverted' (i.e. with hills as holes) try turning the page round (90 degrees at a time) until the topography looks correct. The human visual system expects shadows to be below rather than above an object, and in the case of Figure 2.7, an anticlockwise rotation of 90 degrees might make things fall into place for you.

Rotating the picture is a trick well worth remembering, because you will be looking at a great many pictures of planetary surfaces as you study this course. Also, you will be expected to recognise a crater when you see one and to use shadows to work out from which direction the illumination is coming.

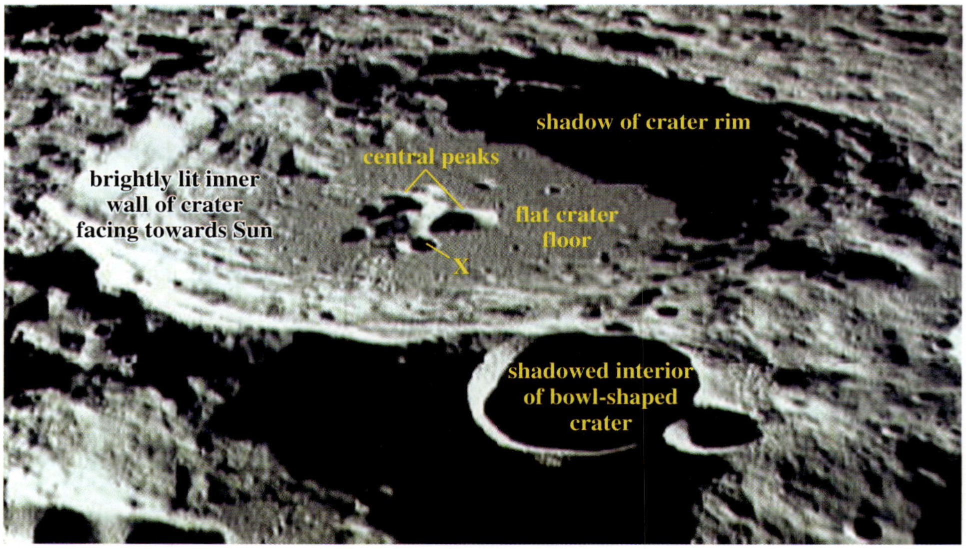

Figure 2.8 An enlargement of part of Figure 2.7. See Box 2.5 for discussion.

Impact craters are particularly easy to see on the Moon (if you have used binoculars or a telescope for Activity 1.2 yet, you will almost certainly have noticed some), but their origin was controversial for a long time. Until the 1960s most people thought they were volcanic features, but now we realize that any resemblance between lunar craters and volcanic craters is merely superficial. Most lunar craters are far more regular in shape (in fact, circular) than volcanic craters (which is because they were excavated by shock waves radiating away from the point of impact), and unlike most volcanoes, the crater floor is lower than the level of the surrounding terrain. Also, crater morphology changes systematically with size: craters less than about 15 km across are simple bowl shapes with raised rims, larger craters have central peaks, even larger ones have a central ring of peaks, and craters that are hundreds of kilometres across consist of concentric rings. The same hierarchy of crater morphology can be seen on cratered surfaces of other planetary bodies, with the transition from one type to another occurring at smaller sizes on bodies with stronger gravity.

On planetary surfaces old enough to have collected a sufficient number of impact craters, counting the number of craters per unit area is the best way we have of estimating the age of the surface. As *TYP* p. 14 explains, we can use this method to determine the absolute age of surfaces on the Moon. It seems to work fairly well elsewhere in the inner Solar System, but by the time we reach the orbit of Jupiter the signs are that the impacting debris is from different sources and that the rates of cratering are not comparable. However, it remains true that, on the surface of any single planetary body, a more densely cratered surface has to be older than a less densely cratered surface.

Many young craters, especially, are surrounded by recognizable blankets of ejecta, which is fragmented material thrown out during excavation of the crater. Because of their finely broken nature, ejecta deposits are often paler than the rest of the surface. Ejecta can be continuous adjacent to a crater, but may take the form of 'rays' radiating outwards at greater distances (you will see examples later in the course). Large blocks of ejecta may strike the surface with sufficient energy to excavate their own craters, which are described as secondary craters. These are perfectly ordinary-looking craters, and can be recognized as secondaries only by association with the main crater. In impacts that form large craters, a very small proportion of ejecta may be flung out with sufficient speed to escape the planet's gravity entirely. A few such fragments originating from impacts on the Moon and Mars have been collected on Earth, where they can be recognized as very unusual meteorites.

2.2.3 Differentiation and the interiors of terrestrial planets

TYP p. 13 introduced the concept of differentiation, which is the process whereby the denser component of a planet's substance sinks towards its centre, and *TYP* Figure 2.5 illustrated the differentiated internal structures of the giant planets. For comparison, though at a different scale, Figure 2.9 shows the interiors of the terrestrial planets.

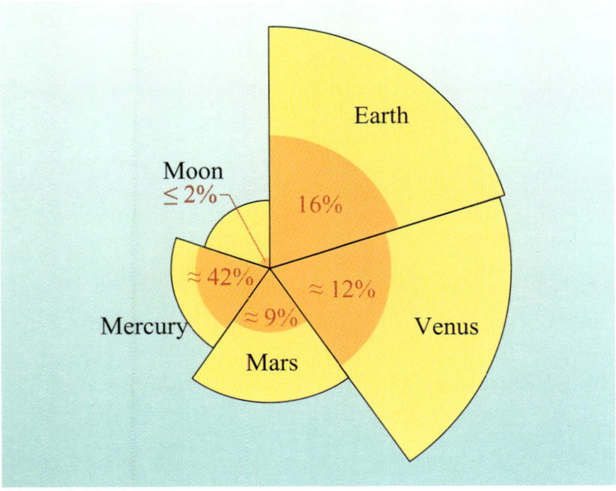

Figure 2.9 Cross-sections to compare the internal structures of the terrestrial planets, with an iron-rich core surrounded by a rocky mantle. The values in red show the percentage of each body's volume occupied by its core.

2.2.4 What qualifies as a planet?

As this course is called *Planets: an introduction* it is worth spending a little time to discuss what we actually mean by the term 'planet'. You may have gathered from Chapters 1 and 2 that it is surprisingly tricky to come up with a watertight definition. A glance at the glossary entry for 'planet' in *TYP* confirms this.

Perhaps the best way to give you a clear picture of the arguments is to state that there is no dispute about those bodies that definitely *are* planets. Our Solar System has eight of these: Mercury, Venus, Earth, Mars, Jupiter, Saturn, Uranus and Neptune. Each of these is considerably larger than any other object in the same region of space, and each of them orbits the Sun. The problem, if that's how you choose to regard it, lies in deciding which, if any, other bodies qualify as planets.

One way of deciding eligibility for planethood is shape. It is reasonable to rule out anything so small that its own gravity is too weak to have pulled it into a near-spherical shape. If we invoke this rule, then none of the asteroids counts as a planet. They still bear the shapes inherited from collisions and fragmentation, and not even the largest ones have smooth round shapes. Today, nobody suggests that any of the asteroids ought to be regarded as a planet, although sometimes they are referred to as 'minor planets'.

Kuiper is pronounced KY-per, with the emphasis on the first syllable.

On the other hand, the status of Pluto has caused a lot of contention. Although large enough to have a near-spherical shape, it is considerably smaller than any of the eight planets previously listed. Furthermore, many other bodies have now been discovered in similar orbits to Pluto, and the largest of them are also nearly spherical and not very much smaller than Pluto. These are the Kuiper belt objects, and there can be no doubt that if Pluto had been discovered in the year 2000 rather than 1930 it would have been classified as the largest known Kuiper belt object rather than as a planet. Few would now disagree with this as an assessment of Pluto's *nature*. However, Pluto was regarded as a planet when it was discovered and this went virtually unchallenged for more than fifty years. The formal situation was made clear in a statement released by the International Astronomical Union (IAU) in 1999. This explained that even though it is now accepted that Pluto is just the largest known example of a different class of bodies it will retain its official *status* as a planet, for historical reasons.

The Moon, with a capital M, means the Earth's natural satellite. When we write moon, with a lower-case m, it means any natural satellite of any body.

What of other possible candidates for planethood within the Solar System? Our own Moon and several satellites of the outer planets are considerably bigger than Pluto. These are not generally regarded as planets because they do not orbit the Sun; rather they orbit a larger planet, which itself orbits the Sun. However, this distinction is drawn from the perspective of an astronomer rather than that of a planetary scientist. If we want to study such things as the role of volcanoes in transporting heat and molten materials to the surface of a large body, or the evolution of a dense atmosphere then the body's orbit is scarcely relevant. Hence the argument on *TYP* p. 14 that the Moon is effectively a fifth terrestrial planet.

In this course, when I need a term that deliberately encompasses definite planets plus some or all of the bodies that are not universally regarded as planets, I use the term 'planetary body'.

I have discussed some of the issues concerned with deciding the *lower* size limit for a planet. Before moving on, I ought to point out that defining the *upper* size limit has recently become an issue too. This is not relevant within our own Solar System, but it does become important when identifying planets around other stars, because many of these are very large and fall in the 'grey area' between objects that are definitely planets and objects that are definitely stars. You will read about this is in Chapter 14 (*TYP* p. 213).

2.2.5 Naming conventions

This is an appropriate place to mention how planetary bodies get their names, and also how their surface features are named. The names of all the planets from Saturn inwards have come down to us from ancient times. In most European languages they bear the names of gods from Roman mythology.

It is the prerogative of the discoverer of a new object to suggest a name. However, in order to become established the name has to win acceptance by the rest of the world. For example, when he discovered Uranus in 1781, William Herschel wanted to call it *Georgium sidus* (which is Latin for 'George's star') in honour of his patron King George III. Herschel obstinately clung to that name all his life, but continental astronomers (and eventually the British too) adopted the more appropriate name Uranus, taken from the Roman pantheon. Later, when Neptune and Pluto were discovered, they were given appropriate names from the same source.

These days it is the duty of various working groups of the IAU to award official names to newly discovered objects, and you will read about this process later in the course (notably in Chapter 8).

Telescopic observers of the Moon and Mars had named many surface features before the coming of the space age began to provide detailed views. These revealed thousands more landscape features to name on these and many other planetary bodies. You may think that it is fairly pointless to give names to places where nobody lives or is ever likely to visit, but a name is much the most convenient way to specify which particular feature we mean when attempting to describe it, or to compare it with another.

The IAU has a set of rules for naming surface features. These specify themes for the names, with the intention that the heritage of all human cultural groups is fairly represented across the Solar System as a whole. For example: names on Mercury reflect artists, musicians, painters, authors, or ships of discovery; names on Venus are of famous women or goddesses; names on Ganymede (a satellite of Jupiter) are taken from the mythology of ancient Egypt and the Middle East.

Most types of feature are given a *descriptor term*, based on a Latin word, as part of their name. Some descriptor terms that you will meet in this course are listed in Table 2.1. Specific examples that you will come across include Santa Maria Rupes on Mercury, Maat Mons on Venus, and Valles Marineris on Mars. Craters are an exception, because they are so common and so many had been named on the Moon before the IAU convention was adopted. These are given names without a descriptor. Thus, almost always when you come upon an unqualified name of a feature on a planetary surface, you can assume it is an impact crater.

Table 2.1 Some common descriptor terms for features on planetary surfaces. You do not need to remember these terms, but you will have to refer back to this table several times later in the course.

Term (plural in brackets)	Meaning
Catena (catenae)	Chain of craters
Cavus (cavi)	Irregular steep-sided depression, usually in a cluster
Chaos	Distinctive area of broken terrain
Chasma (chasmata)	Deep, elongated, steep-sided depression
Corona (coronae)	Ovoid feature
Facula (faculae)	Bright spot
Fluctus (fluctus)	Flow-like feature
Fossa (fossae)	Long, narrow, shallow, depression
Labyrinthus (labyrinthi)	Complex of intersecting valleys
Linea (lineae)	A dark or bright elongate marking, may be curved or straight
Macula (maculae)	Dark spot
Mensa (mensae)	Flat-topped prominence, with cliff-like edges
Mons (montes)	Mountain
Patera (paterae)	Irregular crater, often with scalloped edges
Planitia (planitiae)	Low-lying plain
Planum (plana)	Plateau or high plain
Regio (regiones)	A large area marked by reflectivity or colour distinctions from adjacent areas, or a broad geographic region
Rupes (rupes)	Scarp
Sulcus (sulci)	Parallel or nearly parallel ridges and furrows
Tholus (tholi)	Small dome-like mountain or hill
Unda (undae)	Dunes (usually used only in the plural)
Vallis (valles)	Valley
Vastitas (vastitates)	Extensive plain

Descriptor terms are intentionally just descriptions of what a feature looks like. They are not intended as explanations of how a feature was formed. This is partly because we are not always sure of the true nature of a feature, and also because it is likely that some features bearing the same descriptor term on different planetary bodies were produced by completely different processes.

2.2.6 Planetary heat

Three sources of heat in the interiors of planetary bodies are mentioned on *TYP* pp. 20–21.

- Primordial heat is the heat trapped within a planetary body during the processes that gave birth to the body, and which is still leaking out (slowly) today. As mentioned on *TYP* p. 13, the source of most of this heat is the energy released during collisions.
- Radiogenic heat comes from decay of natural radioactive substances; you do not need to know more about this process than is said on *TYP* p. 21.
- Tidal heating is a result of tidal distortion of a body's shape. *TYP* does not say much about tidal forces. You are probably aware that both the Sun and the Moon raise tides in the Earth's oceans. All you need to appreciate about tides affecting the solid parts of planetary bodies is that when a small body orbits a more massive body, the side of the small body closer to the massive body experiences a stronger gravitational force (because it is closer) than the side farther from the massive body. As a result, the shape of the smaller body is slightly distorted.

2.2.7 Planetary facts

Subsequent chapters of *TYP* begin with a table of planetary facts. You do not need to remember the information in these tables, but you will need to be able to retrieve and understand the meaning of this information. *TYP* pp. 21–23 define the meaning of each of the entries for these tables.

One thing not explained anywhere in *TYP* is that every planetary body with a solid surface has a conventionally recognized system of latitude and longitude, analogous to that used on the Earth. The equator is simply defined as lying mid-way between the poles of rotation. On a body with prograde rotation, the north pole is the one pointing in roughly the same direction as the Earth's north pole. Longitude is defined relative to a north–south line on the surface whose position has been chosen by the IAU. Sometimes there is no independent reason for the choice of location of this line defining zero longitude. For example, the line of zero longitude on the Earth (the Greenwich meridian) has no special significance – it simply ended up being the international standard (rather than a line running through Paris) because the British were able to out-argue the French.

2.2.8 Still worried?

I have tried to offer additional explanation for all the important aspects of this chapter that I think may worry you, especially if you are new to science. If there is anything bothering you that I have not elaborated here, then the chances are that lack of understanding is unlikely to prevent your successful study of this course. However, remember that you can ask your Study Advisor for additional explanation or clarification. It can also be useful to consult the computer-based course conference: check first to see whether there is already any discussion of the issue, and if not start it going yourself. In this situation, for example, if the difference between prograde and retrograde has you flummoxed, then post a message entitled something like 'prograde and retrograde?' and containing a plea for help such as 'Has anybody got a good way of visualizing and remembering the difference between prograde and retrograde, because I still can't get my head round it!' It is likely that either a fellow student or another contributor to the conference will reply with a helpful idea.

2.3 Chapter 2 questions

Now try to answer the following questions, to remind you of some of the things you have learned and test your understanding of them.

Question 2.5

A more precise value of the mass of the Earth than the value quoted in Box 2.1 is $5.973\,698\,992 \times 10^{24}$ kg. (a) To how many significant figures is this precise value quoted? (b) Express the value correctly to five significant figures. (c) Express the value correctly to eight significant figures. ◀

Question 2.6

Mercury's orbital period is quoted in days in *TYP* Table 2.1. Without cheating (by converting straight from days into fractions of a year), feed Mercury's average distance from the Sun (as given in this table) into Kepler's third law of planetary motion to calculate its orbital period in years. (For the final stage of your working out you will have to use the square root key on your calculator, which will probably be indicated by the mathematical square root symbol √ or by SQRT.) ◀

Question 2.7

In planetary science, what specific meaning does the term 'differentiation' have? Select one answer from the list.

A Distinguishing a planet from an object that is not a planet

B The process whereby the interior of a planetary body has become segregated into layers of different composition

C The growth of planetesimals in the solar nebula

D Determining composition by means of spectroscopy ◀

Question 2.8

Which of the following is a correct and complete listing of our Solar System's giant planets? Select one answer from the list.

A Jupiter and Saturn only

B Jupiter, Saturn, Uranus and Neptune

C Jupiter, Saturn, Uranus, Neptune and Pluto

D Mercury, Venus, Earth, Mars, Jupiter, Saturn, Uranus and Neptune ◀

Question 2.9

Which of the following is *not* a process that can contribute to the heat in the interiors of planetary bodies? Select one answer from the list.

A Radioactive decay

B Tidal forces

C Spectroscopy

D High velocity collisions ◀

Question 2.10

Which of the following would *not* be correct use of a descriptor term for naming a feature on a planetary surface? Select one answer from the list.

A Caloris Planitia – for a low-lying plain

B Nightingale Corona – for a large oval feature

C Kepler – for a crater

D Pavonis Mons – for a volcano

E Noctis Vallis – for a network of intersecting valleys ◀

Mercury

3

Now study *TYP* Chapter 3, remembering to highlight the key parts of the text as you go along. This deals with the planet Mercury, and is structured in the same way as the next ten chapters. However this chapter is fairly short, because we know relatively little about Mercury, and it has no satellites. Return here when you have finished Chapter 3.

3.1 Discussion of Chapter 3

3.1.1 The relationship between Mercury's rotation and orbit

The *Rotation and orbit* section (*TYP* pp. 25–26) describes the way in which Mercury's rotation has become tidally locked into a relationship with its orbital period. It states that the 3 : 2 ratio between orbital period and rotation period means that Mercury's day is twice as long as its year, and invites you to puzzle this out for yourself. This is quite tricky. The key to it is that 'rotation period' means the spin of a planet on its axis measured *relative to the Universe as a whole*, not relative to the Sun (as already pointed out in Section 2.1.3). If you were standing on a planet that was not rotating, you would nevertheless experience one sunrise and one sunset (i.e., one local day) during each orbit around the Sun, because the planet's orbital motion would make the Sun's position appear to migrate round the sky. Conversely, if you were on a planet that rotated (in the prograde direction, i.e., rotating in same sense as its orbital motion) exactly once per orbit, the Sun would not appear to move around the sky at all; one hemisphere of the planet would continuously face the Sun and the other would be in perpetual darkness.

The actual situation for Mercury, which rotates one and a half times in the prograde direction during each orbit, is illustrated in Figure 3.1.

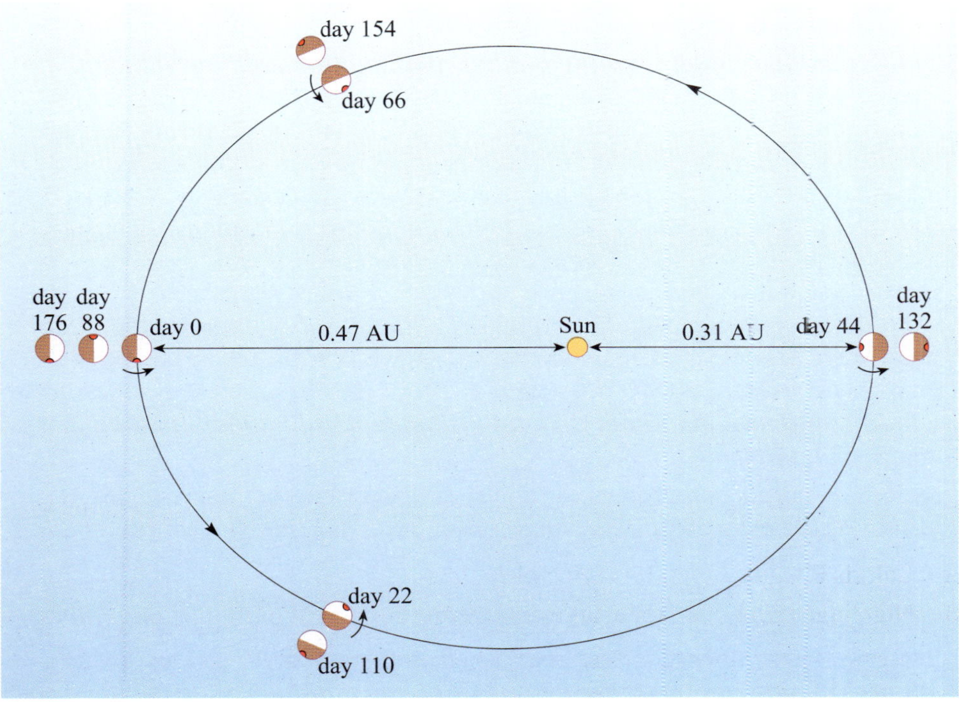

Figure 3.1 The relationship between Mercury's rotation and orbit. Mercury's location and rotation are illustrated every quarter of an orbit, as the planet moves around two complete orbits. The dot identifies a fixed point on the planet, which rotates three times during these two orbits in the direction indicated. On day 0 the dot is experiencing sunrise, on day 88 it is experiencing sunset, and at day 176 it is experiencing sunrise again, which means that the length of a day on Mercury is 176 Earth-days. To avoid superimposing the pictures, Mercury's position has been drawn as if displaced outwards on successive orbits. The sizes of both Mercury and the Sun have been exaggerated, and in fact Mercury is much smaller than the Sun.

In Figure 3.1, why has Mercury travelled less than a quarter of the way around its orbit by day 22, even though 22 days is a quarter of Mercury's orbital period?

This is a consequence of Kepler's second law of planetary motion, which means that a planet travels slower when farther from the Sun.

3.1.2 The rest of Chapter 3

The rest of Chapter 3 is a discussion of Mercury from the perspective of a planetary scientist interested in Mercury as a world in its own right, rather than as an object orbiting the Sun. There are some questions below to help you assess whether you have understood what you read there. But first, a few comments and further explanation:

- The rather surprising presence of ice at Mercury's poles (*TYP* p. 27) has not been proven; it is merely the only credible explanation that anyone has yet come up with to account for the peculiar radar reflections. It will be an important goal of future missions to Mercury to attempt to verify whether or not this is correct. You will discover in Chapter 6 that there is rather more complete evidence for dispersed polar ice near the Moon's poles.
- You have presumably heard of radar. In planetary science this relies on transmitting a sort of radio signal from an antenna on the Earth or on a spacecraft and analysing the signal bounced back (reflected) from a planetary surface. It is not important for this course that you understand any more than that. The radar reflections indicative of ice on small areas of Mercury are described on *TYP* p. 27 as 'polarized'. That term refers to a property of the reflected radar beam that is beyond the scope of this course.
- You will find magnetic fields discussed for many planetary bodies in this course. The important thing to know is that for a body to generate a strong magnetic field its interior must include a zone that is fluid, a good conductor of electricity, and in motion. It is important to distinguish between a magnetic field that is being *generated* within a planetary body and one that has been inherited from the past and is 'locked in' to the rocks. Such a 'remanent' magnetic field is much weaker, and can only be stored by magnetic minerals at temperatures less than about 580 °C.
- If you consult textbooks outside this course, you may find some that state that Mercury has no atmosphere, in apparent contradiction to *TYP* p. 29. That is fair enough actually. The atoms of hydrogen, sodium, helium and potassium that have been detected above Mercury's surface do not constitute an atmosphere in the conventional sense of a shroud of gas retained by the planet's gravity. What is described as Mercury's atmosphere in *TYP* is atoms that are continually leaking away (and presumably being replenished at the same rate). It is far too tenuous to experience familiar atmospheric phenomena such as winds and clouds. If you look at the *Planetary facts* table for Mercury on *TYP* p. 25, you will see that the atmospheric pressure at Mercury's surface is shown as 10^{-15}, relative to the atmospheric pressure at the Earth's surface. This is another example of scientific notation, which was introduced in Box 2.1. Consult Box 3.1 for a discussion of this strange-looking number.
- There are abundant impact craters on all the pictures of Mercury shown in this chapter. As the text points out, this shows that Mercury's surface is very old. The age cannot be uniform because some areas have relatively few craters and so must be younger. However, even the youngest tracts of surface probably date back to about three billion years ago. The Caloris basin (whose formal name is Caloris Planitia) is described as a multiringed impact basin, and is an example of the concentric ring structure described for craters hundreds of kilometres across in Section 2.2.2.

- The pictures of Mercury in this chapter are referred to as 'images' and never as 'photographs'. This is because they were recorded and transmitted digitally, and photographic film played no part in their acquisition. Not all textbooks make this distinction, and elsewhere you may find the term 'photograph' bandied about rather carelessly. In this course I have tried to use 'photograph' only for pictures taken by astronauts using film. See Box 3.2 for an examination of a digital image.

Box 3.1 More scientific notation, and orders of magnitude

Mercury's atmospheric pressure is quoted as 10^{-15} that of the Earth (we could write it more fully as '1×10^{-15}', but the '$1 \times$' is redundant). In this case the power of ten is preceded by a minus sign, and it means that the number is 1 divided by 1 followed by 15 zeros (i.e. 1 divided by 10^{15}, or $1/10^{15}$, which is 0.000 000 000 000 001). That makes a very small number indeed. We can describe Mercury's atmospheric pressure as being 15 orders of magnitude less than the Earth's.

A value that is about ten times smaller than another is described as one order of magnitude smaller, about a hundred times smaller is described as two orders of magnitude smaller, etc. Turning this round, we can equally speak of one value being so many orders of magnitude greater than another. Values that differ by less than an order of magnitude are described as being 'of the same order of magnitude'. For example, 400 and 600 are of the same order of magnitude (as each other), and so are 9×10^3 and 2.5×10^4. Even though in the second case the two values have different powers of ten, the larger value is in fact less than three times greater than the smaller one.

Incidentally, you would say 10^{-15} as 'ten to the minus fifteen' and 10^{15} as 'ten to the fifteen'.

Box 3.2 A digital image

Digital images are recorded electronically, rather than on photographic film. If you own a digital camera for taking family snapshots, this discussion should contain much that is familiar.

The information that makes up a digital image consists of a string of numbers, each of which represents the brightness of a tiny patch of the image. These tiny patches, which are usually square, are called 'picture elements' or 'pixels'. Most of the digital images used in this course consist of nearly a million pixels each. In the case of an image of a planetary surface, the distance across the area of ground covered by a pixel is often spoken of as representing the 'resolution' of the image. A high-resolution image shows fine detail by virtue of its small pixels. Each pixel in a low-resolution image covers a larger area and so the image does not show so much detail.

Normally, when you look at a digital image you do not notice the individual pixels. However, if a portion of an image has been greatly magnified, as in the example on the right of Figure 3.2, then the pixels become apparent. If you look at this from across the room, it may seem unremarkable, but as you bring it closer to your eyes its appearance will break up into a mass of little grey squares.

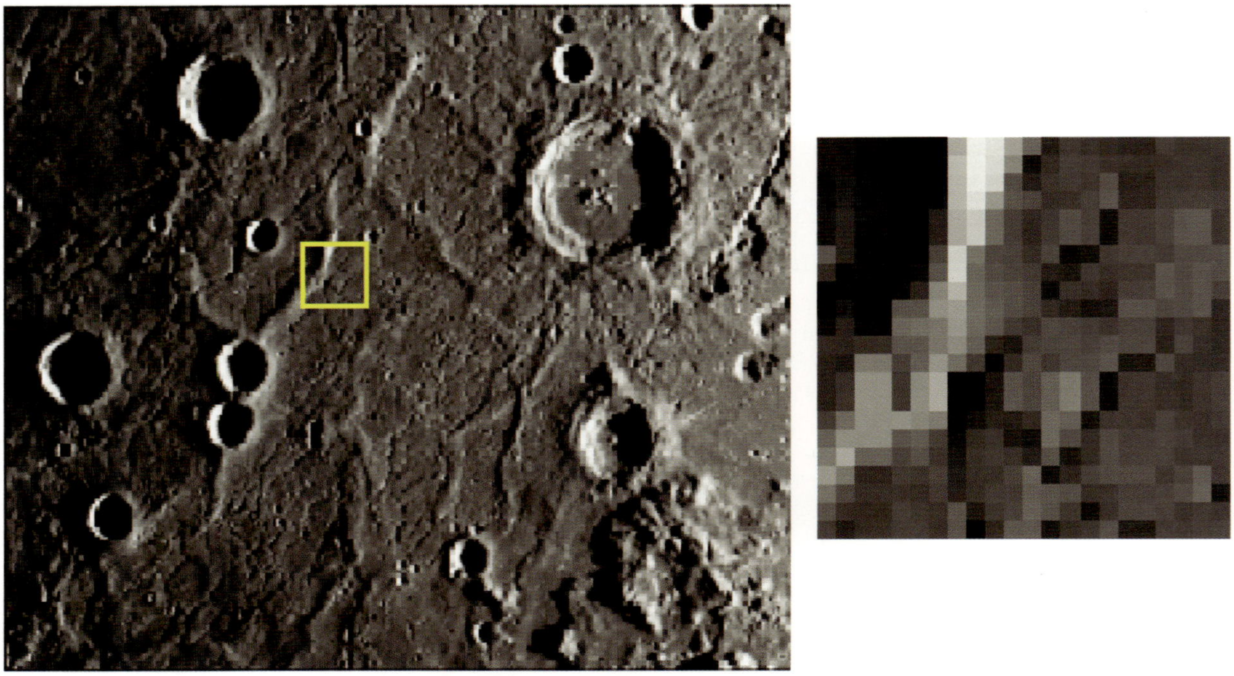

Figure 3.2 A digital image (reproduced from *TYP* Figure 3.4). The area within the yellow box is shown enlarged on the right. This magnification reveals the individual pixels of which the image is composed.

Question 3.1

Bearing in mind what you learned in Box 2.5, can you deduce (a) which way the sunlight is coming from in Figure 3.2, (b) whether the long feature that cuts through the top left part of the box in Figure 3.2 is a ridge or a valley, (c) which way the sunlight is coming from in *TYP* Figure 3.5? ◀

TYP p. 31 mentions colour information in the Mariner 10 images. As the course progresses, you will see several examples of images recorded in different parts of the spectrum that have been cleverly combined in colour. Mariner 10 was not very well equipped for this; however, it recorded some images of the same area through different filters, and a processed example is shown in Figure 3.3. See Box 3.3 for information on the spectrum.

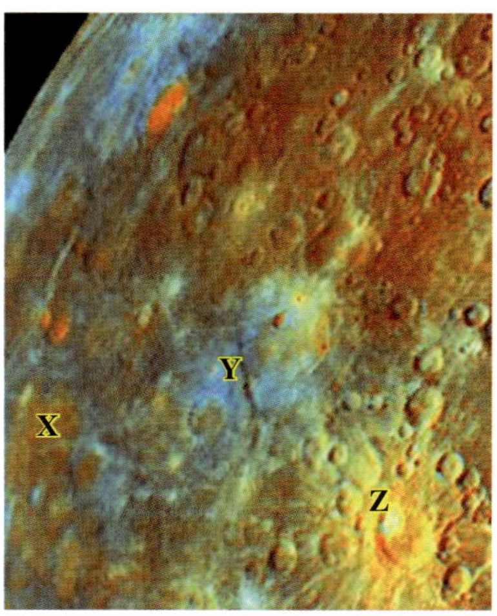

Figure 3.3 A false-colour Mariner 10 image of a 1000 km wide area of Mercury. Colours have been designed to exaggerate areas poor in opaque minerals in red, and iron-rich or more recently exposed surfaces in green. The ratio between ultraviolet and orange light controls the blue component. In this image, the dull red area surrounding X is probably a field of lava flows, the blue area surrounding Y is interpreted as ejecta from ancient impacts, and the bright yellow splash near Z marks the relatively young (perhaps 1 billion year old) 60 km impact crater named Kuiper.

Box 3.3 The spectrum and coloured images

The light to which your eyes are sensitive is electromagnetic radiation, but you can see only a small part of the full spectrum (Figure 3.4). Electromagnetic radiation consists of electrical and magnetic vibrations travelling at the speed of light. This radiation is usually described in terms of the distance between successive peaks in the vibration, which is known as the wavelength.

Visible light ranges in wavelength from 400 nm (violet) to 700 nm (red). Wavelengths too short for you to see are described as ultraviolet (even shorter wavelength radiation is called X-rays), and wavelengths too long for you to see are described as infrared. At even longer wavelengths we reach the regions known as microwave and radio. Most spacecraft record images in the visible and the closely adjacent parts of the ultraviolet and infrared. Many images you will see reproduced in black and white were recorded by gathering light across a large part of this range, but some were recorded across a narrow wavelength range using a colour filter.

In Box 3.3, the abbreviation nm stands for nanometres. A nanometre is 10^{-9} of a metre, which is a millionth (10^{-6}) of a millimetre.

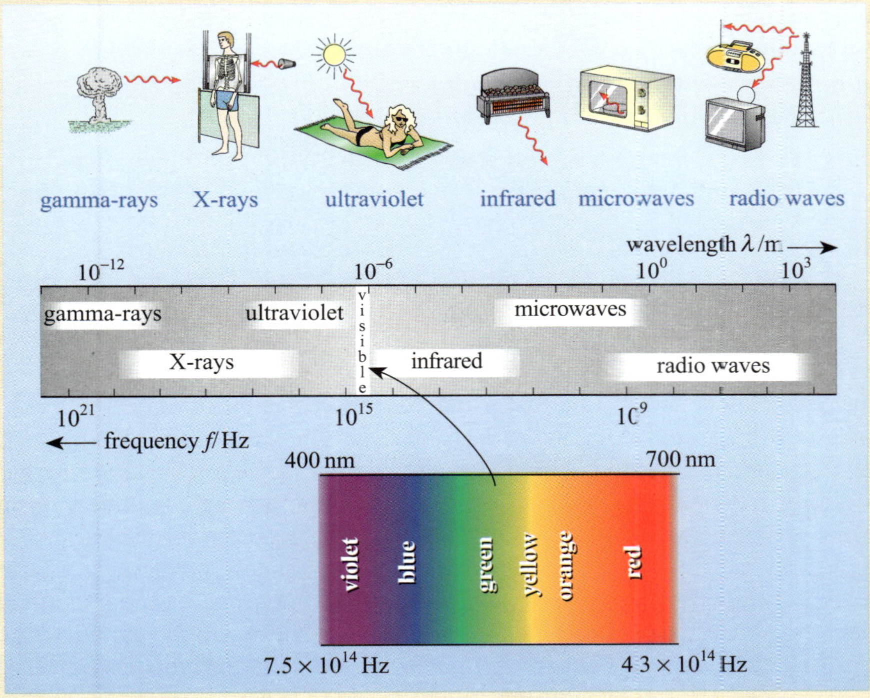

Figure 3.4 The electromagnetic spectrum, showing how visible light is only a tiny proportion of the whole.

The simplest way to get a colour image is to combine images from three wavelengths by showing one in red, one in green and one in blue. The resulting colours will be 'natural' only if the wavelengths recorded were actually red, green and blue, and even then the colours can be artificially exaggerated or 'enhanced' to reveal subtle variations. Often, the input to the red, green and blue components of an image do not correspond to these wavelengths; they can come from invisible parts of the spectrum, or can be ratios between wavelengths (as, for example, used in Figure 3.5). When something like this has been done, the image is said to be in 'false colour'.

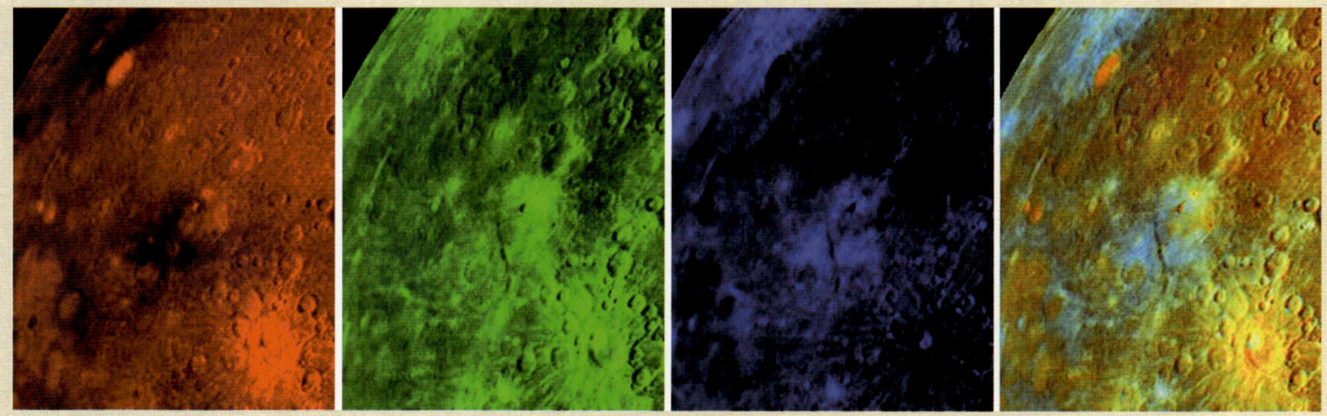

(a) (b) (c) (d)

Figure 3.5 How a colour image is constructed, by combining separate, but coincident, images in red, green and blue: (a) red input, (b) green input, (c) blue input, (d) the combined image, which in this case is the one used in Figure 3.3.

Infrared wavelengths greater than about 3000 nm are more useful for recording emitted radiation (because of a body's heat) rather than reflected radiation, and are sometimes referred to as thermal infrared. Beyond the infrared region, at wavelengths greater than a millimetre, we reach the microwave region that is used by radar.

In Figure 3.4, wavelength has been drawn on a non-linear scale, with each division being a power of ten greater than the previous one, in order to display the range conveniently. Such a scale is described as 'logarithmic', but you need not worry about that in this course. Frequency, measured in the unit abbreviated Hz (standing for hertz, and meaning vibrations per second), is inversely related to wavelength, and is something else that need not concern you.

- The day–night boundary runs just within the left-hand edge of *TYP* Figure 3.2, and you will notice that the closer you look to this boundary, the longer the shadows (because, bearing in mind the curvature of the globe, the closer to this boundary, the lower the Sun appears in the sky). The day–night boundary on an image of a planet is referred to as the 'terminator'. The craters in the left of *TYP* Figures 3.2 and 3.4 are almost completely filled by shadow, not because they are necessarily any deeper than the craters to the right, but because the curvature of Mercury's surface means that the Sun gets lower in the sky as the terminator is approached. If you look back at Figure 1.3 you will see that Galileo correctly drew more prominently visible topography near to the lunar terminator.
- The scarp named Santa Maria Rupes runs across *TYP* Figure 3.5. *Santa Maria* is the name of the ship on which Columbus first sailed to the Americas, and so this is consistent with the 'ships of discovery' naming convention for many of the features on Mercury mentioned in Section 2.2.5.

3.2 Chapter 3 Activities

There are two Activities for this chapter. The first is another chance to check your highlighting. The second is designed to introduce you to the use of the S196 CD-ROM. To warn you that you need your CD-ROM (and, of course, your computer) we show an appropriate symbol in the margin.

Activity 3.1 More highlighting

(*The estimated time for this Activity is 10 minutes.*)

Have you been highlighting *TYP* while you read it? I am not going to keep going on about it, but it will probably help your study if you do so. If you have been highlighting, turn to the discussion of this Activity on page 111 to see how I would choose to highlight the final paragraph of *TYP* p. 28. If you have not highlighted any of Chapter 3, please re-read that paragraph in *TYP* and decide what the key points are before comparing your analysis with my highlighting example.

Activity 3.2 Using the S196 CD-ROM

(*The estimated time for this Activity is 50 minutes.*)

Open your S196 CD-ROM on your computer. Refer to the loading instructions in Appendix 2 of the *Study Guide* if you are unsure how to do this.

When you have opened the Main Menu screen, click on the 'Planets' button to reach a screen with a list of planetary bodies, grouped together in a logical fashion. Each name is within a button that you can select by clicking on it with the pointer controlled by your mouse. If you click on a button you will be taken to a screen containing up to ten small 'thumbnail' images, beside a title and the first few words of a caption. At the bottom of the screen there may be an option to advance to the next ten pictures of the same planetary body, and when you get there you will have the option to go back to the previous ten or forwards to the next ten (if available). To get back to the general image archive screen, just click on the words *Image Archive* at the top of the screen, or on adjacent square button.

If you click on either the 'thumbnail' or the title of an image, you are taken to a larger and more detailed version of the image, usually accompanied by a descriptive caption. To get back to the index page from any of these, you simply need to click on the button that appears near the lower right corner of the image.

Please explore the *Image Archive* now by clicking on the blue rectangular button labelled 'Mercury'. This will take you to a screen of ten 'thumbnails', bearing the text *Mercury 1-10* at the top right. Click on the first of these (Merc1). You may recognize that this is *TYP* Figure 3.1. However, details are more clearly visible than in the printed version. You will generally find it is the case that the first images for each planetary body in this archive are based on *TYP* Figures. There is a short caption to the right of the image, and a longer caption below it that you can get to either by scrolling down or clicking on the underlined words <u>*Go to full text*</u> that appear at the lower right. These captions are a general feature of images on this CD-ROM. I wrote some of them myself, but others have been copied from NASA sources. The latter may reflect preliminary interpretations only, and may not use terms so clearly and consistently as in the rest of the course materials.

Now get back to the *Mercury 1-10* screen. The quickest way is to use your browser's 'back' button. Alternatively, you can click on the square button at the lower right of the current image, which will take you to the general image archive screen. When you are back at the *Mercury 1-10* screen, click on the second 'thumbnail' (Merc2). This is a nice clear view of the eastern half of the Caloris basin (*TYP* Figure 3.2). Note the short caption to the right of the image. The words *hemispheric image* here are underlined, which is a signal that if you click on these you will be taken directly to an image showing a whole hemisphere. Try it. You will find that in this case the link has taken you back to Merc1.

Now get back to the *Mercury 1-10* screen, and click on the sixth 'thumbnail' (Merc6). This takes you to a mosaic of images assembled to cover much of Mercury's southern hemisphere. Below the caption on the right are the underlined words *click here to view a large version of this image*. Try it. This takes you to a wonderfully detailed view that is far too large to fit on your screen. Instead, you can roam around it by means of the scroll bars at the edge and bottom of the screen. The button to return you to the main index page is at the lower left corner.

Now get back to the *Mercury 1-10* screen, and click on the word *Next>>* that appears at the bottom right of the screen (you may have to scroll down to find this). This takes you to a screen labelled *Mercury 11-13*. You can examine any of these in the same way as Merc1-Merc10 from the previous screen.

Finally, please go back to the Main Menu screen (you can get there quickly by clicking on the words 'Image Archive' at the top left of any thumbnail screen), and click on the long grey rectangular button labelled 'Keyword Search'. This will open a new window that gives you the opportunity to type any term you like into a small window (at top left). Try this by typing *impact crater* and then clicking on the 'Search' button to the to the right. This will bring up thumbnails of the first ten of over 60 images from the archive whose title or caption includes the term 'impact crater'. The 'Keyword Search' can be a very useful tool for finding examples of comparable features or processes on different bodies.

That is the end of the tour, and you have seen most of the features that the CD-ROM has to offer. I suggest you spend a few minutes exploring the Mercury images before finishing. You will need to examine one of these to answer Question 3.5. There are a fewe comments about this Activity on page 112.

3.3 Chapter 3 questions

Now try to answer the following questions, to remind you of some of the things you have learned and test your understanding of them.

Question 3.2

Why do you think I did not give hints on finding and identifying Mercury in Activity 1.3? ◀

Question 3.3

TYP Figures 3.4 and 3.5 show areas sufficiently similar in size for us to be able to make a comparison between them. Which of the two areas is the more heavily cratered, and what does this tell you about the relative ages of the surfaces? ◀

Question 3.4

Which two of the following statements about Mercury are *not* correct? Select two answers from the list.

A Relative to the size of the planet, Mercury's core is thought to be larger than the Earth's.

B Some effects of the impact that caused the Caloris basin can be seen on the far side of the globe.

C Santa Maria Rupes may have been produced as a result of expansion of the globe.

D Mercury's rotation period is twice as long as its year.

E The floor of the Caloris basin may have been flooded by lava. ◀

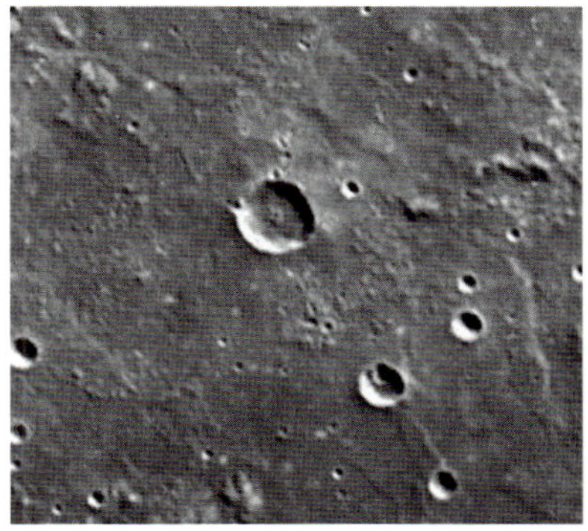

Figure 3.6 An image of part of Mercury, showing an area a few hundred kilometres across. For use in Question 3.5.

Question 3.5

Examine Figure 3.6. Which direction is the illumination coming from: top, upper right, right, lower right, bottom, lower left, left, upper left? ◀

Question 3.6

Locate image Merc12 on the S196 CD-ROM. There is a 140 km diameter crater dominating the right-hand side of this image. Study the appearance of this crater, and, with reference to Section 2.2.2, identify from the list below two features that this image does *not* reveal.

A Central peak

B Bowl-shaped morphology of the main crater

C Terracing on inner wall

D Secondary craters

E Ejecta rays

◀

4 Venus

Now study *TYP* Chapter 4 (don't forget about highlighting!). This deals with Venus, and, for good reasons, is somewhat longer than the previous chapter. Return here when you have finished Chapter 4.

4.1 Discussion of Chapter 4

This chapter was similar in structure to the previous one. However, although they are both terrestrial planets, there are significant differences between Mercury and Venus. Most notable are the younger age of Venus's surface and the density of its atmosphere. You will also have noted that this atmosphere is opaque to visible light, so that all the images of the surface recorded from above the atmosphere have been obtained using radar.

Here are some comments and further explanation. Read these before doing the Activity and attempting the questions.

- Venus's rotation is defined as retrograde because it spins in a clockwise direction as seen from above the Sun's north pole. This is in the opposite direction to its orbital motion. It is conventional to quote axial inclination (the angle of a planet's spin axis) as less than 90° for prograde rotation and between 90° and 180° for retrograde rotation, hence the value of 177.4° in the *Planetary facts* table on *TYP* p. 35.
- *TYP* Figure 4.1 shows the top of Venus's cloud layer recorded through a violet filter. Images recorded using the full range of visible light do not show so much detail. However, ultraviolet light (even shorter wavelength than violet; see Figure 3.4) reveals the cloud structure even more clearly, as you can see if you examine images Venus15 and 16 on the S196 CD-ROM.
- The processing required to generate a radar image is complicated, but it is not necessary for you to understand any more about imaging radar than is said on *TYP* p. 38 in the *Missions to Venus* section. Remember, though, that a radar image is generated by analysing reflection of a (broad) beam shining obliquely onto the surface, whereas radar altimetry (for measuring the height of the topography) uses a (narrow) beam shining vertically downwards.
- The greenhouse effect is introduced on *TYP* p. 39 in *The atmosphere*. However, no explanation is given of why carbon dioxide acts as a greenhouse gas but nitrogen does not. In fact, the reason is that in order to be a strong absorber of infrared radiation (and hence able to act as a greenhouse gas by trapping heat), each molecule needs to consist of at least two atoms of *different* elements. A molecule of the most abundant gas in the Earth's atmosphere, nitrogen, consists of two identical atoms of nitrogen, and so does not absorb infrared radiation. It has the chemical formula N_2, in which N symbolizes an atom of nitrogen. On the other hand, a molecule of the most abundant gas in the atmosphere of Venus, carbon dioxide, consists of one atom of carbon bonded to two atoms of oxygen, which makes it a strong absorber of infrared radiation, and hence a highly effective greenhouse gas. This has the chemical formula CO_2, in which C represents an atom of carbon and O represents an atom of oxygen. The term 'dioxide' in the name indicates two oxygen atoms.

- Water has the chemical formula H_2O, which signifies that each molecule of water consists of one atom of oxygen bonded to two atoms of hydrogen. Do you think the presence of water vapour in a planet's atmosphere would contribute to the greenhouse effect, and why?

- A water molecule meets the necessary condition of consisting of at least two atoms of different elements, and so water vapour is a greenhouse gas. It is particularly important in this role in the Earth's atmosphere because of its relative abundance, but it also contributes to the greenhouse effect on Venus and Mars.

- Water vapour could have been the cause of a runaway greenhouse effect early in Venus's history, leading to evaporation of any oceans and subsequent breakdown of water molecules in the upper atmosphere. Photodissociation, the breakdown of molecules exposed to solar radiation (especially ultraviolet), is a process that you will meet several times in this course.
- *TYP* p. 42 mentions interpretations of the thickness of Venus's crust based on mapping the planet's gravity field. You will find similar discussion of planetary interiors several times in this course, but you do not need to understand how gravity mapping works.

- What is meant by the term 'crust' when referring to a terrestrial planet, and how does it differ from both 'mantle' and 'lithosphere'? Refer back to *TYP* pp. 13–14 if you can't remember.

- The crust is the outermost, chemically distinct layer. It overlies the mantle, but both are essentially rocky (silicate) in composition. The lithosphere is a mechanically defined layer consisting of the crust plus the rigid part of the mantle, and overlies the deeper, convecting, part of the mantle known as the asthenosphere. (You could also have obtained this answer by looking up the terms in the Glossary near the back of *TYP*.)

- The topography of Venus is illustrated in *TYP* Plate 1. The two hemispheres are printed rather small, but you can find much larger versions as images Venus19 and 20 on the S196 CD-ROM, and (conveniently) you can swap from one to the other simply by clicking on the image. It is important to remember that the colour is completely artificial, and is just used as a way of indicating the height of the surface.
- *TYP* Figure 4.3 shows a remarkable view recorded in visible light by a lander on the surface of Venus. The S196 CD-ROM has a colour version of this as image Venus3 (do not worry if you do not understand the technical terms in the long version of the caption, which was originated by NASA).
- The sections entitled *The surface* and *Global history* (*TYP* pp. 43–53) contain a lot of information. Activity 4.1 and Questions 4.4–4.5 are intended to reinforce and test your understanding of what is covered there.

4.2 Chapter 4 Activity

In *TYP*, only Figures 4.6 and 4.10 show impact craters on Venus. This activity shows you some more examples.

Activity 4.1 Craters on Venus

(The estimated time for this Activity is 20 minutes.)

The final paragraph of *The surface* (*TYP* p. 51) mentions how Venus's dense atmosphere protects the surface from small impactors, because they are slowed down and worn away by atmospheric drag. Figure 4.1 illustrates some consequences of the fragmentation of impactors before they reached the surface.

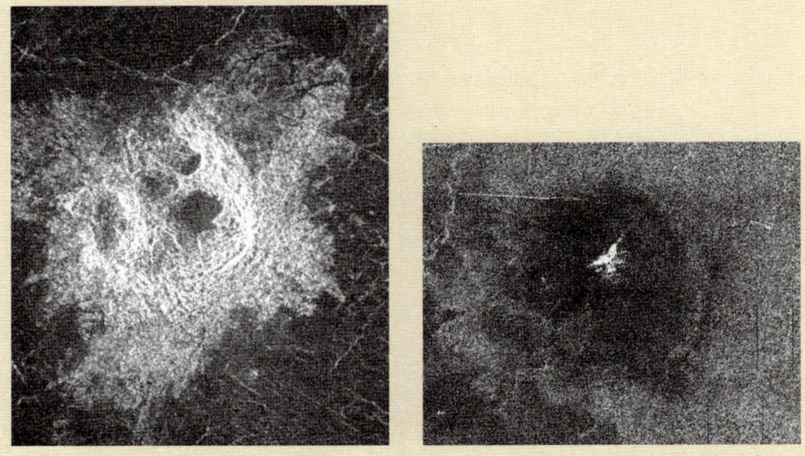

(a) (b)

Figure 4.1 (a) A 30 km wide portion of a Magellan radar image showing a cluster of four craters thought to result from an impactor breaking apart just before it hit the surface. (b) An 80 km wide portion of a Magellan radar image showing a surface blemish believed to be produced by an impactor that became almost completely fragmented within the atmosphere. The radar-dark (i.e., smooth textured) blotch probably shows where the surface was pulverized by the atmospheric shock wave, and the radar-bright (i.e., rough) feature in its centre shows where surviving fragments of the impactor hit the surface but at speeds too slow to excavate proper craters.

You may be able to see more on the versions of these two images that appear as images Venus21 and 22 on the S196 CD-ROM. Please look at these now, and also the other crater images Venus23-26. Venus23 and 24 show a fairly typical Venus crater called Golubkina in a conventional radar image and a perspective view made by incorporating altimetric data. The natures of the raised rim, terraced inner wall, low-lying crater floor and central peak are particularly apparent in the perspective view. Venus25 shows a crater sufficiently large that instead of a central peak it has a ring of peaks (described as a peak-ring). Venus26 shows a rare example of a crater on Venus that has been partly destroyed by surface deformation (in this case by faulting).

4.3 Chapter 4 questions

Now try to answer the following questions, to remind you of some of the things you have learned and to test your understanding of them.

Question 4.1

Which reason from the list is likely to be the correct explanation of why Venus does not generate a strong magnetic field?

A It is too hot.

B It is rotating too slowly.

C It has no core.

D Its interior contains no fluid zone. ◀

Question 4.2

The Venus *Planetary facts* table on *TYP* p. 35 lists five gases in Venus's atmosphere. Which of these would contribute to the greenhouse effect, and why? ◀

Question 4.3

In the first paragraph of *TYP* p. 41, it is suggested that the atmospheres of Venus and the Earth originated 'by volcanic degassing'. Referring back to *TYP* p. 20 if necessary, can you work out what is meant by this term? ◀

Question 4.4

Look at image Venus12 on the S196 CD-ROM. As the caption describes, this shows two flat-topped domes ('pancake domes') believed to have been formed by extrusions of viscous lava. Bearing in mind the simple information about apparent brightness of features on radar images that is given in *Missions to Venus* (*TYP* p. 38); decide (a) from which direction the radar beam was coming (look at the western dome in particular), and (b) how rough the dome tops are compared with the terrain upon which the domes are built. ◀

Question 4.5

Look at the image in Figure 4.2. In the light of examples you saw while studying this chapter, how would you interpret (a) the pale surface occupying most of the western (left-hand side) half, (b) the pale surface occupying much of the eastern (right-hand side) third? ◀

Figure 4.2 A 300 km wide Magellan image of part of the surface of Venus. North is towards the top. For use with Question 4.5.

Question 4.6

On the basis of what you have learned by studying this chapter, which one of the following statements about Venus is likely to be correct?

A Channels cutting across the surface were probably cut by flowing water.

B The mantle below Venus's lithosphere is probably getting warmer.

C Impact craters are usually associated with smooth, radar-dark ejecta beyond their rims.

D The abundance of impact craters varies greatly from place to place across the globe. ◀

5 The Earth

Now study *TYP* Chapter 5. This deals with the Earth, and I hope you will find it thought-provoking to see the Earth described at similar length to its fellow planets. Return here when you have finished Chapter 5.

5.1 Discussion of Chapter 5

5.1.1 The relationship between the Earth's rotation and orbit

The Earth's day-length (exactly 24 hours, by definition) differs from its rotation period (23 hours 56 minutes, according to *TYP* p. 55) for exactly the same reasons why Mercury's day-length (176 Earth-days) is longer than its rotation period (58.6 Earth-days). If you are still puzzled by this, it may help if you refer back to Figure 3.1, but remember that the Earth rotates many more times per orbit than Mercury does.

The chapter assumed that you are aware of the causes of the seasons, or that you could work it out from the brief description given on *TYP* p. 56. In case you are still puzzled, Figure 5.1 ought to clear up any problems you may have in visualizing the seasons. Note that Figure 5.1 is drawn as if from a different vantage point in space to the one used in Figure 2.2b.

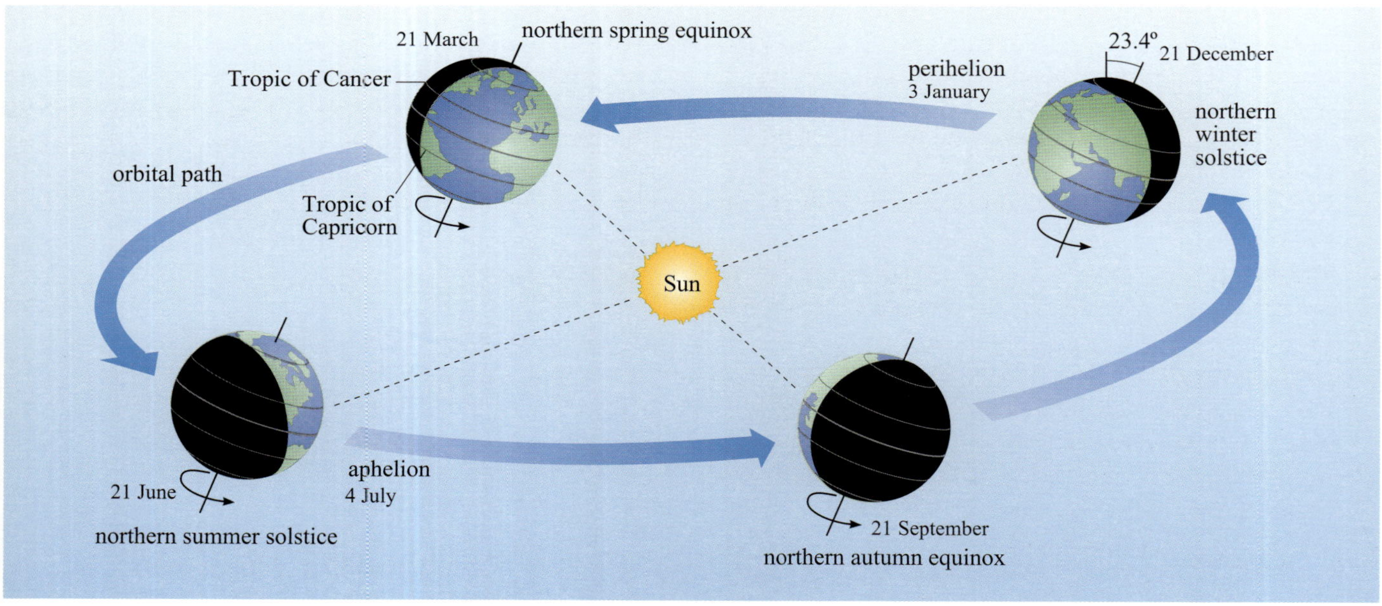

Figure 5.1 The seasons related to Earth's orbit round the Sun. The direction of the Earth's axis is inclined at 23.4° to the orbital plane and does not change perceptibly during the course of a year. At the time of the northern winter solstice, the north end of the axis is tilted most fully away from the Sun, so it is winter in the northern hemisphere and summer in the southern hemisphere. On this date the Sun is above the horizon round the clock at latitudes less than 23.4° from the south pole, is overhead at the Tropic of Capricorn (23.4° south of the Equator) at midday, and does not rise above the horizon at points closer than 23.4° to the north pole. Conversely, at the time of the northern summer solstice, the north end of the axis is tilted most fully towards the Sun, so it is summer in the northern hemisphere and winter in the southern hemisphere. At the equinoxes, the axial tilt is neither towards nor away from the Sun, and there are exactly 12 hours between sunrise and sunset at every point on the globe.

What to the terms 'perihelion' and 'aphelion' signify on Figure 5.1?

According to the definitions on *TYP* p. 9, perihelion must indicate the point where the Earth's orbit is closest to the Sun whereas aphelion indicates the most distant point.

At present, perihelion occurs a few days after the northern winter solstice and aphelion shortly after the northern summer solstice. This is coincidental, and the slight change in the Earth–Sun distance associated with this has nothing to do with the seasons.

The seasons are of course responsible for the differences in weather and temperature experienced at different times of the year. Longer term climate change is a least partly driven by slow changes in the amount of the inclination of the axis and in the eccentricity of the orbit. You will discover in Chapter 7 that similar phenomena probably drive climate change on Mars.

5.1.2 The rest of Chapter 5

Read the following comments and explanation before doing the Activity and answering the questions.

- Unlike (so far as we can tell) what has happened on any other planetary body in the Solar System, the composition of the Earth's atmosphere and hence the surface temperature (thanks to the greenhouse effect) have been strongly influenced by the development of a complex biosphere of living organisms.
- The system of Hadley cells illustrated in *TYP* Figure 5.1 that transports heat away from the Equator and towards the poles is something that the Earth has in common with most planets that have substantial atmospheres. A simpler pattern with fewer cells was described for Venus in the previous chapter, and as the current chapter points out the difference is essentially because of the Earth's more rapid rotation. You will find Hadley circulation described later in the course for Mars, Jupiter and Saturn.
- The clouds in the Earth's atmosphere are formed by tiny suspended droplets of water, except the highest clouds, which are tiny icy crystals.
- Thanks mainly to seismic data, our knowledge of the sizes and properties of the layers in the Earth's interior is far superior to what we know, or can infer, about interiors of other planetary bodies. The Moon is the only other planetary body for which we have any seismic information at all, and this is much less complete than for the Earth. However, even for the Earth the exact cocktail of elements occurring in the core is a matter for speculation.
- The action of plate tectonics plus the surface erosion caused by wind, flowing water and glaciers means that almost all of the Earth's surface is relatively young.

5.2 Chapter 5 Activity

There is only one image of the Earth from space in *TYP*. This activity shows you many more examples.

Activity 5.1 The Earth seen from space

(The estimated time for this Activity is 30 minutes.)

During this course you will see images of impact craters on virtually all the major planetary bodies in the Solar System. Impact craters are rare on the Earth's surface, because the rates at which they are removed by erosion or hidden by burial almost keep pace with the rate of formation. However, impact craters are not completely unknown on Earth. There are images of three of them as Earth12-14 on the S196 CD-ROM, which you should now look at. Earth12 is a small and relatively young crater, only about 50 000 years old. Being so young and in a fairly arid part of the globe, it has suffered little erosion. In contrast the much larger craters in Earth13 and Earth14 are hundreds of millions of years old. These two examples are in tectonically stable (i.e., not prone to deformation) areas that are also free of volcanic activity, otherwise such old craters would be unlikely to have survived on the Earth. Even so they have suffered considerable erosion so that we no longer see the original crater topography. Incidentally, note that Earth14 is a radar image acquired in the same way as Magellan's radar images of Venus, but with artificial colour added. Other craters that have become buried beneath thick layers of sediments have been discovered by detailed seismic and gravity surveys. A famous example is the 200 km Chicxulub crater on the coast of the Yucatan peninsula in Mexico. This is the largest known of several 65 million year old craters whose origin is probably associated with events that led to a mass extinction of many kinds of life (including the dinosaurs). Here the crater is buried under 1.5 km of sediments, and there is very little sign of it from space, as images Earth15 and 16 demonstrate. However, it can be revealed by mapping the local variations in gravity, which reflect variable density in the sub-surface rock, as Figure 5.2 shows.

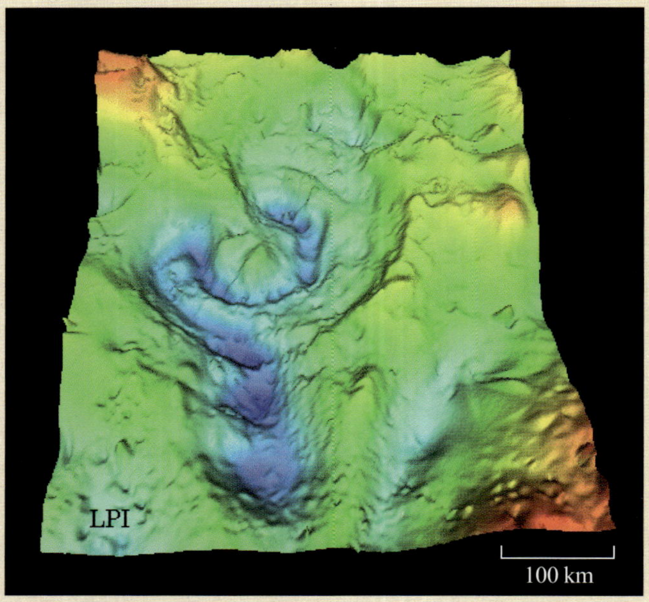

Figure 5.2 Computer-generated three-dimensional perspective view of sub-surface density derived from mapping gravity variations. The Chicxulub crater is the 200 km diameter circular region of low density (blue–green). The 90 km diameter ring of slightly higher density corresponds to a peak-ring (which is expected for a crater of this size). The green 'peak' in the centre represents dense rocks below the crater rather than a real central peak.

Other Earth images on the S196 CD-ROM include global views showing cloud patterns (Earth1-10), volcanic eruptions (Earth17-20), non-erupting volcanoes (Earth21-25), rotating weather patterns (Earth27-30), rivers (Earth31-40), ice sheets and glaciers (Earth43-48), mountains (Earth49-52), arid areas (Earth53-57), and some views recorded on or close to the surface (Earth60-63). You may enjoy browsing through these. For this course it is not important to spend much time on this. However, if you do browse through these pictures consider how incomplete and inadequate an impression you would get of the Earth if these images were all you had to go on, and try to bear that in mind when you are looking at images of other planetary bodies.

5.3 Chapter 5 questions

Now try to answer the following questions, to remind you of some of the things you have learned and test your understanding of them.

Question 5.1

Which property of the Earth from the list, as compared with Venus, is *not* likely to be a simple consequence of its rapid rotation?

A Rotating weather systems

B Days much shorter than the year

C The division of the lithosphere into tectonic plates

D More complex pattern of Hadley cells

E Much stronger magnetic field ◀

Question 5.2

Which statement about the Earth in the list is correct?

A The action of plate tectonics allows the crust to slide across the mantle that directly underlies it.

B All volcanoes occur near plate boundaries.

C Oceanic crust is produced by melting of continental crust.

D The Earth's continental crust ceased to grow about 2500 million years ago.

E The outer part of the core is liquid. ◀

Question 5.3

In what ways does the Earth's present atmosphere differ in composition from the original atmosphere that was released by volcanic degassing? ◀

6 The Moon

Now study *TYP* Chapter 6. This deals with the only planetary body that everyone is familiar with seeing in the sky. It will help if you have been able to carry out Activity 1.2 by now, but don't worry if you haven't. Return here when you have finished Chapter 6.

6.1 Discussion of Chapter 6

Read the following comments and explanation before answering the questions.

- As is the convention for satellites, the Moon's rotation period is defined in the *Planetary facts* table (*TYP* p. 66) relative to the planet that it orbits rather than relative to the universe as a whole. This is a different convention from the one adopted for planets themselves.
- The Moon's synchronous rotation enables the line of zero longitude to be defined on a logical principle, in contrast to the arbitrary basis used on the terrestrial planets (Section 2.2.7). Lunar zero longitude is defined as running centrally across the Moon's Earth-facing hemisphere. The same principle is used to define zero longitude on synchronously-rotating satellites of other planets.
- *TYP* p. 67 mentions Kepler's second law of planetary motion in connection with the Moon's orbit round the Earth. Although originally formulated to describe the motion of a planet about the Sun, Kepler's laws also describe the motion of a satellite around any other body. Beware though that you cannot use Kepler's *third* law to relate orbital periods of bodies that do not orbit the same central body, because the orbital period depends on the mass of the central body. The constant k in Equation 2.1 has the value 1 only if the orbit is around the Sun. It will have a smaller value for orbits around a less massive body (such as a planet or a low-mass star), and a higher value for orbits about a star more massive than the Sun.
- The evidence for ice near the lunar poles is stronger than that for ice on Mercury, where we have only radar reflections using signals transmitted from the Earth. For the Moon there are two sorts of useful data, both of which were collected from lunar orbit: radar reflections detected by Clementine over the south pole (*TYP* p. 67), and the neutron signature detected by Lunar Prospector over both poles (*TYP* p. 68). You are not expected to understand how the neutron signature is derived, or why it indicates ice. You can see the specific locations where Clementine indicated ice on image Moon6 on the S196 CD-ROM, if you click on the words click here in the caption.
- In case you were wondering, *maria* (meaning 'seas', and used only for regions on the Moon) is not pronounced like the girl's name. You should say 'MAH-ree-a'. The singular, *mare*, should be pronounced 'MAH-ray'.
- *TYP* pp. 70–71 point out that almost all the lunar surface is covered by a layer of fragmental material (regolith) resulting from meteorite impacts. *TYP* Figure 6.3 does not give a terribly clear impression of this, so take a look at Figure 6.1. The variety of fragment sizes is apparent, as well as the ability of the regolith to retain the imprint of a booted foot. You can also gain a good insight into what it is like on the lunar surface by looking at the panoramas that are provided as Moon34-45 on the S196 CD-ROM. Clicking and dragging with your mouse on these images lets you look around in any direction, and even to peer down towards your feet a bit. Even if you do not look at much else on the CD-ROM, be sure not to miss out on these marvellous and eerie views.

- Figures in *TYP* Chapter 6 illustrate lunar craters as small as the 300 m Elbow crater in the top right part of *TYP* Figure 6.6. Figure 6.2 here shows a 40 m crater named Plum. Younger craters less than a metre across are clearly visible where sunlight falls at a grazing angle onto the inner slope of Plum in Moon26 and 27 on the S196 CD-ROM.

(a)

(b)

Figure 6.1 (a) Sampling small stones from the lunar regolith using tongs during the Apollo 12 mission. Note also that the astronaut has just kicked up a spray of dust with his right boot. (b) A scoop used to collect a regolith sample during the Apollo 17 mission, though obviously the rock beside the scoop is too large to fit.

Figure 6.2 A panoramic view of Plum crater, which is about 40 m in diameter. This is in the lunar highlands and was visited by Apollo 16 astronauts in April 1972.

- It was once widely assumed that lunar craters are a result of past volcanic activity. This concept was well and truly debunked from the 1960s onwards by new understanding of the impact process (*TYP* Figure 2.4), and by recognition of impact craters on all ancient surfaces in the Solar System and at all scales. In fact, very few recognisable craters on the Moon are volcanic.
- *TYP* pp. 74–75 describe long, winding valleys interpreted as collapsed lava tubes that indicate the paths along which lava flowed to fill the mare basins, but only one example (Hadley Rille) is illustrated (*TYP* Figure 6.6). This photograph is part of the panorama that you have as Moon41 on the S196 CD-ROM. It is unlikely that the lava tube explanation for such features on the Moon would have been dreamt up, unless similar (though smaller-scale) features were already known on the Earth. Unless you are very lucky, you are unlikely to have seen one of these, so Figure 6.3 shows you an example.

Figure 6.3 A 4 m wide lava tube in Hawaii. Left: a view looking along the collapsed tube. Right: an arch where part of the roof has survived collapse.

- Because their origin as lava tubes cannot often be proven, it is more usual to refer to these as rilles. There are several rilles visible in Moon25 on the S196 CD-ROM. It is well worth examining this image, because it conveys a lot of information about lunar history.

  - How can you tell that the large crater (Prinz) in the left foreground of Moon25 is older than the large crater beyond it (Aristarchus).

  - Prinz was clearly formed before this region became covered by mare basalts. It *became largely flooded by* these basalt lava flows which overtopped its rim on the far side. Conversely, Aristarchus (and its associated ejecta blanket) can be seen to have been formed *on top of* the mare basalts. You might also note the considerable number of small impact craters on the mare surface within Prinz, whereas few or no such craters are visible within Aristarchus or on its ejecta blanket, which demonstrates that Aristarchus post-dates most of the cratering that has affected the mare surface.

6.2 Chapter 6 questions

Now try to answer the following questions, to remind you of some of the things you have learned and test your understanding of them. When you have finished these, you will have completed about a third of the estimated total study time required for this course. That would be a good time to take stock of whether your rate of progress so far has been appropriate for you to complete the course in time for to meet your target ECA submission date (see the S196 *Study Guide* Section 3.7).

Question 6.1

The first sentence of *The atmosphere and polar ice* (*TYP* p. 67) describes the Moon's atmosphere as 'almost as insubstantial as Mercury's'. Use the atmospheric pressure data in the *Planetary facts* tables of Chapters 3 and 6 (*TYP* p. 25 and p. 66) to calculate how the Moon's atmospheric pressure compares with Mercury's in terms of orders of magnitude. [Refer to Boxes 3.1 and 6.1 if you need help.] ◀

Box 6.1 Multiplying and dividing powers of ten

When we multiply two numbers expressed in scientific notation, the rule is to multiply the numbers but *add* the powers of ten.

To calculate $A \times 10^f$ *multiplied* by $B \times 10^g$ we simply work out $A \times B \times 10^{f+g}$ (note that we *add* the powers).

So, for example $3 \times 10^6 \times 5 \times 10^3 = 3 \times 5 \times 10^{6+3} = 15 \times 10^8$ (which we could express as 1.5×10^9 if we want to make the number before the × take a value of between 1 and 10)

On the other hand, to calculate $A \times 10^f$ *divided* by $B \times 10^g$ we simply work out $(A \div B) \times 10^{f-g}$ (note that we *subtract* the powers).

So, for example $3 \times 10^6 \div 5 \times 10^3 = 3/5 \times 10^{6-3} = 0.6 \times 10^3$ (which we could express as 6×10^2 if we want to make the number before the × take a value of between 1 and 10).

You will find further examples and explanation in Boxes 6.1 and 6.2 of the booklet *Background material on maths skills*.

Question 6.2

Look at the basic properties of the Moon listed in the *Planetary facts* table (*TYP* p. 66). Which of these do you think is likely to exert the greatest influence on the ease with which liquid lava can flow on the Moon relative to its behaviour on the Earth? ◀

Question 6.3

Which statement about the Moon in the list is correct?

A Apollo seismic data show that the Moon's lithosphere is on average about 70 km thick.

B The Moon's core is thought to be at least 1290 km across.

C The lunar highlands are older than the maria.

D There are no lava flows on the Moon.

E The outer part of the core is liquid. ◀

7 Mars

Now study *TYP* Chapter 7. This deals with Mars, which is the outermost of the bodies conventionally classified as terrestrial planets. Return here when you have finished Chapter 7.

7.1 Discussion of Chapter 7

Read the following comments and explanation before answering the questions. Many of the comments indicate helpful images on the S196 CD-ROM.

- Mars has been the target for a great many space missions. *TYP* Table 7.1 lists only the successful ones, plus some that still lay in the future when *TYP* was prepared. As you may be aware, planetary scientists and engineers based at the Open University have played a major role in developing and securing funding for the Beagle 2 Mars lander. If you have Internet access you can find out more about the progress of this project at http://www.beagle2.com. If not, Figure 7.1 should give you a sufficient impression of the plans for the mission.

  - The Beagle 2 landing site is near the centre of a feature called Isidis Planitia. 'Planitia' is a descriptor term that is part of the name but which, as explained in Section 2.2.5, conveys information about the nature of the feature. Using Table 2.1 (p. 26) to help you, what kind of place would you expect Isidis Planitia to be?

  - The term 'Planitia' denotes a low-lying plain.

In fact, Isidis Planitia is a large lowland basin cut into the edge of the highlands, and is near the centre of the globe in the upper right of *TYP* Plate 4. It may have originated as a large impact basin like Hellas (described on *TYP* pp. 83–84), but it has a long subsequent history of sedimentary infill and small-scale volcanism. Image Mars48 on the S196 CD-ROM shows one of many lines of probable volcanic cones on the floor of Isidis Planitia. There are also impact craters of various ages (some of them partly buried by sediment) and fields of small pale sand-dunes (notably where the near-surface wind appears to have been focused through a gap in the line of cones).

Some people write Martian, others martian without a capital letter. Most Open University courses opt for the latter, which is consistent with lunar and solar.

- Mars has been studied from Earth using telescopes for a long time. The polar caps and some surface albedo patterns can be recognized, but the spacecraft images used to illustrate this chapter show much more detail than can be seen from Earth. Although Mars does have some large canyons, these do *not* coincide with the martian 'canals' first reported by a telescope observer in 1877, which turned out to be optical illusions and not real at all. *TYP* Figure 7.2 is one of the best ever views of Mars from Earth, and this was recorded using a telescope in orbit above the Earth's atmosphere.
- Substantial caps of ice at the poles are a feature that Mars shares with the Earth and Triton, a satellite of Neptune that you will learn about in Chapter 12. *TYP* p. 82 and p. 92 both mention the layering exposed at the edges of the martian polar caps. Rather than being annual seasonal layers these probably reflect longer term cycles of climate change. A highly detailed view of this layering is shown as Mars9 on the S196 CD-ROM. [See Box 7.1 for an explanation of the term 'to sublime', which is used on *TYP* p. 80.]

Figure 7.1 Simulated views of some crucial stages in the Mars Express mission. (a) Approach of the spacecraft to Mars in December 2003. (b) Separation of the Beagle 2 lander from the Mars Express craft, five days before the latter enters orbit about Mars. Beagle 2 weighs 65 kg and is less than a metre in diameter when still folded away inside its entry capsule. (c) Beagle 2 deployed on the martian surface. (All Rights Reserved Beagle 2)

Box 7.1 Sublimation

Under most familiar circumstances, if you heat a solid it will turn to liquid, and more heat needs to be applied to turn it to vapour. Melting frozen water and then boiling it is the most familiar example. However, under appropriate conditions solids can go directly to vapour without melting first. 'Dry ice', the substance used on stage to generate clouds of mist, is frozen carbon dioxide, and at room temperature on Earth this turns directly to vapour without melting. This process is called sublimation, and the solid carbon dioxide is said to 'sublime' when it turns into vapour.

The factor that determines whether a solid will melt or sublime on heating is the atmospheric pressure, or rather the contribution of the vapour from the particular substance to the total atmospheric pressure. Carbon dioxide is unstable in liquid form unless confined by carbon dioxide gas (vapour) at a pressure of several times the Earth's total atmospheric pressure. On Mars the pressure is far lower than this, which is why frozen carbon dioxide in the polar caps sublimes directly to vapour when it is warmed by the Sun.

In order for water to be stable as a liquid, the pressure of water vapour in an atmosphere must exceed about a hundredth of the Earth's total atmospheric pressure. This condition is not met today on Mars, so warming frozen water in its polar ice would cause it to sublime rather than to melt. However, Mars could have had a denser and more water-rich atmosphere at various times in the past, which would have enabled liquid water to be stable under surface conditions.

- The dust storms on Mars have been famous for quite a while, because when a large one is in progress it can hide those surface features that would otherwise be visible from Earth using a telescope. A very nice example of a small martian dust storm is shown as Mars42 on the S196 CD-ROM.
- *TYP* p. 80 also describes clouds and mists. Figure 7.2 shows an example, and additional pictures of clouds and mist are shown as Mars13 and Mars49-52 on the S196 CD-ROM.

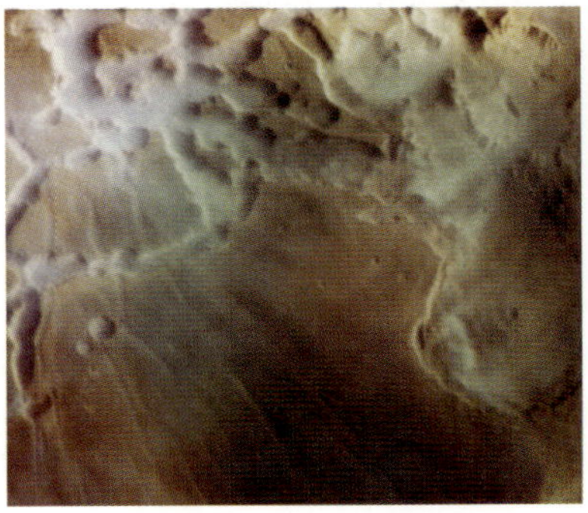

Figure 7.2 Early morning mist in the canyons of Noctis Labyrinthus, generated as sunlight evaporates ice that had condensed overnight on the canyon walls. This view is about 360 km across and is of an area immediately south of the one in the left of *TYP* Figure 7.8.

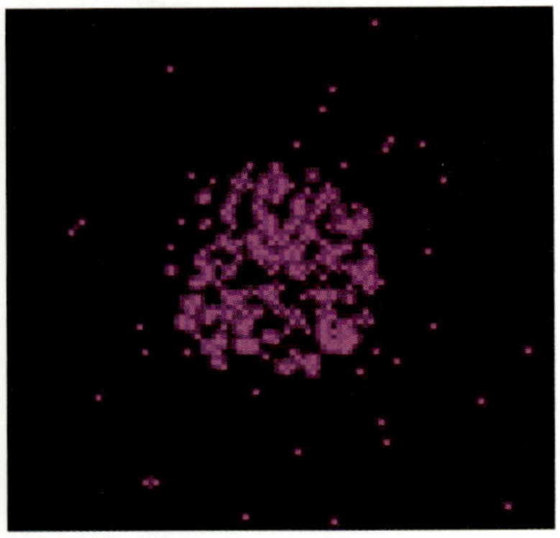

Figure 7.3 A whole-disc view of Mars recorded by the Chandra X-ray Observatory in orbit about the Earth. The image is a record of X-ray fluorescence in Mars's thermosphere, caused by absorption of higher energy solar X-rays.

- This course does not say much about the outer limits of planetary atmospheres. There is no sharp edge to any atmosphere, but by about 100 km altitude the atmospheres of Venus, the Earth and Mars are several orders of magnitude less dense than at the surface and are exposed to the effects of short wavelength solar ultraviolet and X-ray radiation. Rather than merely breaking molecules apart (photodissociation), this particularly short wavelength radiation strips electrons away from the atoms in the atmosphere (it 'ionizes' them). It also adds heat to the atmosphere, so this outer region of an atmosphere is called the thermosphere (the lowest part of this is often referred to as the 'ionosphere', a term you may have heard of because of the influence of the Earth's ionosphere on radio communication). Despite being so tenuous, the thermospheres of Venus, the Earth and Mars stop any radiation shorter than about 100 nm wavelength (about a quarter the wavelength of blue light) from penetrating any deeper. A remarkable image of the martian thermosphere is shown in Figure 7.3.
- If you turn back to *TYP* Figure 4.2 (p. 40) you will be able to identify the thermospheres of Venus, the Earth and Mars by the deflection in each atmospheric temperature profile that begins at about 100 km altitude. The comparatively higher temperature of the Earth's thermosphere is a consequence of the greater concentration of oxygen, which absorbs much more heat than carbon dioxide. (This is not the same as the greenhouse effect, which occurs lower in the atmosphere by absorption of infrared radiation emanating from the solar-heated surface; see Section 4.1.)

Can you suggest why there is such a strong contrast between the day and night temperatures in Venus's thermosphere? [Refer to the Venus *Planetary Facts* table on *TYP* p. 35.]

Venus rotates much more slowly than the Earth and Mars, so the thermosphere, which can be heated only on the daylight side of the planet, has plenty of time to cool down overnight.

- The remarkable magnetic stripes in part of the martian highlands can be seen in Mars57 on the S196 CD-ROM, and global topography is strikingly revealed in the rotating animation in Mars63, which was made from the same data set as the colour-coded topography pictures in *TYP* Plate 4.
- *Global topography* (*TYP* pp. 83–85) mentions three factors that disturb the simple pattern of northern plains and southern highlands. These are all illustrated on the S196 CD-ROM. The Hellas basin is shown in Mars31. The Tharsis bulge and its volcanoes are illustrated in Mars13, which you may already have looked at as an example of clouds. The enormous and complex trough system called Valles Marineris is shown in Figure 7.4 (repeated as Mars24), and Mars25 shows a simulated oblique view along part of this trough.

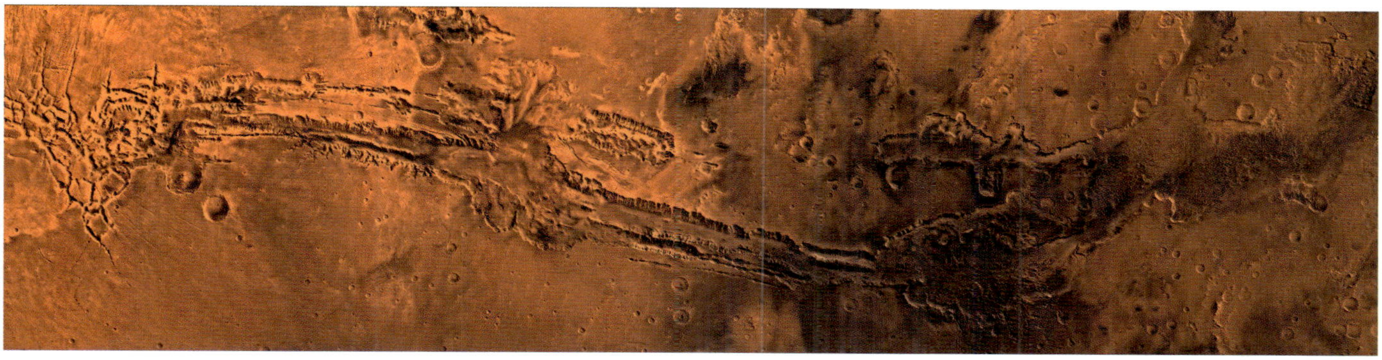

Figure 7.4 A view of Valles Marineris, covering an extent of over 3000 km from east to west.

- *The surface* (*TYP* pp. 85–91) describes various smaller scale features. Views from various landers on the martian surface can be seen on the S196 CD-ROM as Mars43-45 and 58. Impact craters appear in many orbiter images on the CD-ROM, but perhaps Mars36 is the most remarkable because it shows partial burial of older craters on the northern plains. *TYP* Figure 7.5 is particularly important, because the lobate ejecta blanket around this crater (and others like it) is powerful evidence for water (probably frozen) in the subsoil. In addition to the images of channels and gulleys in *TYP*, others are shown as Mars22, 25 and 26. Dunes are seen from orbit in Mars10, 38, 39 and 53-55, and in the view from the Viking 1 lander in Mars58. Volcanoes are featured in Mars15, 17, 19 and 20, suspected small volcanoes are shown in Mars47 and 59, and detailed views of lava flows are shown in Mars16, 18 and 59.
- The young gullies (*TYP* Figure 7.7) on Mars are problematical. Water ice should sublime rather than melting, because liquid water cannot survive under Mars's current low atmospheric pressure (Box 7.1). The explanation could be that this liquid water was unstable, and would have been 'boiling' away even as it flowed. It could not have survived long, but could have come out in a sufficient rush to erode a gully before completely vaporizing. Furthermore, if the roof of the flow froze, this ice-lid would have protected the liquid from vaporization. The larger and much more ancient channel systems (*TYP* Figure 7.6) could be explained as very much larger versions of the same phenomenon, but may also indicate that Mars had a much denser atmosphere at that time.

- Another possible explanation for the small young gullies (which was proposed after I had finished preparing your edition of *TYP*) is that they are sites where water has flowed beneath a capping of snow that fell when the climate was different from today's. On this theory, some of the fallen snow still survives, discoloured by dust, which makes it hard to recognize.
- *Life on Mars* (*TYP* pp. 92–93) highlights the main reason why, at a time of shrinking budgets for Solar System exploration, Mars continues to be a target for so many new missions. There is a combination of important factors: evidence for recent water flow, such as in *TYP* Figure 7.7; the curious properties of the martian meteorite ALH84001 (Figure 7.5); and the relatively recent recognition of the range of apparently hostile environments within which terrestrial organisms can exist.

(a)

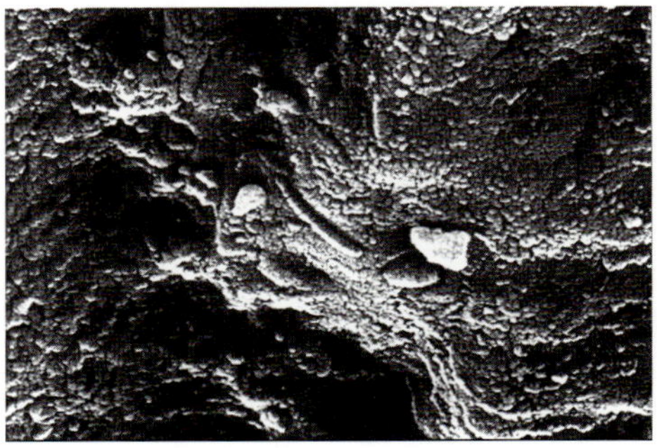

(b)

Figure 7.5 (a) A chunk of the meteorite catalogued as ALH84001 that was found in Antarctica in 1984. It appears to have been dislodged from Mars about 16 million years ago, and arrived on the Earth about 13 thousand years ago. The rock itself is very old, about 4.5 billion years, but reacted with water about 3.6 billion years ago at which stage various chemical indicators of life became trapped within the rock. (b) Although almost certainly *not* fossilized martian bugs, the curious cylinders revealed in this electron microscope view of the interior of this rock prompted much speculation when they were discovered. The view is less than 0.1 mm across.

What mechanism, according to *TYP*, is thought to account for the ejection of rock fragments from Mars, so that they can become meteorites able to strike the Earth?

They are believed to have been flung out as ejecta during impacts that formed large craters (see *TYP* pp. 85–86). Only a tiny proportion of ejecta escapes from Mars, and of this only a tiny proportion reaches the Earth.

- It is not entirely inconceivable that a few microorganisms could survive chance passage from one planet to another within meteoritic ejecta fragments. Terrestrial life could therefore have reached Mars from the Earth. Conversely, and maybe less likely, life on Earth could be descended from microorganisms that came from Mars!

- The two satellites of Mars are tiny objects, and remained undetected until 1877. They are almost certainly captured asteroids, and, if so, they have more in common with the tiny outer satellites of the giant planets than with the Moon or the large satellites of the giant planets. There are several close-ups of both Phobos and Deimos on the S196 CD-ROM.

7.2 Chapter 7 questions

Now try to answer the following questions, to remind you of some of the things you have learned and test your understanding of them.

Question 7.1

According to Table 2.1, which one of the following would *not* be a correct name for features on Mars that you have read about?

A Hellas Planum, for the Hellas basin

B Vastitas Borealis, for the northern lowlands

C Alba Patera, for a volcano with an irregular-shaped summit crater

D Abalos Undae, for a field of dunes ◀

Question 7.2

What mechanism for causing cyclic global climate fluctuations does Mars have in common with the Earth, but possess to a stronger degree? ◀

Question 7.3

Examine *TYP* Figures 7.5, 7.6 (left) and 7.6 (right). In each case, bearing in mind the information given in the captions, deduce from which direction the solar illumination is coming. In case these Figures are not sufficiently clear in the book, you can also find them on the S196 CD-ROM as Mars37 and Mars21. ◀

Question 7.4

Examine Mars18 on the S196 CD-ROM. Can you find any impact craters, and if so what shapes do they have? Using craters and any other visual clues, deduce from which direction the solar illumination is coming. ◀

8 Asteroids

Chapter 8 deals with a family of bodies of which even the largest members are too small to qualify as planets. Nevertheless they are of considerable significance. Many are believed to be little-changed samples of the same material as the planetesimals from which the terrestrial planets were assembled. Asteroids are thought to constitute between 50 and 90% of the objects responsible for the craters visible in the inner Solar System, so it is important to understand whether most are solid lumps or just heaps of loosely bound rubble that would be liable to break apart during passage through a planet's atmosphere. Now study *TYP* Chapter 8, and return here when you have finished.

8.1 Discussion of Chapter 8

Please work your way through the following discussion and questions, before attempting the questions in Section 8.2.

8.1.1 Rotations and orbits

The reasons why some orbits in resonance with Jupiter's orbital period have been swept clear of asteroids, whereas other orbital resonances are well populated, are complex and are beyond this course. *TYP* p. 98 mentions the 3 : 2 resonance as being occupied by a fair sized family of asteroids. Even more have orbital periods near the 7 : 2 resonance.

Question 8.1

(a) Jupiter's orbital period is 11.86 years. Work out the orbital period of a body in (i) 3 : 2 orbital resonance (to do this multiply Jupiter's period by 2 and divide the result by 3), and (ii) a body in 7 : 2 orbital resonance.

(b) Which of the asteroids listed in *TYP* Table 8.1 has an orbital period closest to one of these resonances? ◀

See Box 8.1 for clarification of how close to a perfect ratio two orbital periods must be in order for the situation to count as orbital resonance.

If you have Internet access and want to find out more about the orbits of Jupiter's Trojan asteroids you can do so at http://www.astro.uwo.ca/~wiegert/etrojans/etrojans.html. You can see illustrations and animations of the remarkable orbit of Cruithne (*TYP* p. 98) at http://www.astro.uwo.ca/~wiegert/3753/3753.html, and of a much smaller (100 m diameter) body, whose orbital motion hugs the Earth's orbit even more closely, on the S196 CD-ROM if you select 'Other Asteroids' and then go to Asteroid12-15. The fascinating shapes of these orbits are a result of the repeated tugs these asteroids receive from the Earth's gravity, but you are not expected to understand the reasons in this course.

The rotation axes of elongate asteroids tend not to run along the long axis of the body's shape, but to be at right angles to it. The rotation of an asteroid is thus rather like that of a sausage being twirled around on a cocktail stick. Figure 8.1 illustrates the rotation of Eros seen from above its north pole, and there is a movie of Eros's rotation seen from closer range on the S196 CD-ROM as Eros20.

Box 8.1 Orbital resonance

Orbital resonance is simple to define (as in the *TYP* Glossary). However, how close the ratio of the orbital periods of two bodies must be to an exact simple value (such as 7 : 2) in order for their orbital periods to qualify as being in resonance depends on factors too complex to go into for this course.

In the case of asteroids, there are none for which Jupiter's orbital period is exactly four times or exactly three times their own (these would be in exact 4 : 1 and 3 : 1 orbital resonance). On the other hand, there are plenty for which Jupiter's orbital period is closer to three and a half times their own than to either of those other values. For such asteroids, the ratio between Jupiter's orbital period and their own is close to 3.5 : 1, which, expressed as whole numbers, is 7 : 2. In this context, any ratio closer to 3.5 : 1 than to 4 : 1 or 3 : 1 counts as a 7 : 2 orbital resonance.

Another way to look at the answer to Question 8.1(b), is that the ratio of Jupiter's orbital period to that of Gaspra is 11.86 : 3.28. This is 3.62 : 1, which is clearly closer to 3.5 : 1 than to 4 : 1, so for most purposes we can regard Gaspra as being in 7 : 2 orbital resonance with Jupiter. Likewise, Vesta's 3.63 year orbital period gives a ratio with Jupiter's period of 11.86 : 3.63, which is 3.27 : 1. This is marginally closer to 3:5 : 1 than it is to 3 : 1, so Vesta just about qualifies as being in approximate 7 : 2 orbital resonance with Jupiter.

In the discussion of the next chapter, you will find that Box 9.1 indicates a much stricter fit to exact ratios to define orbital resonance in the context of tidal heating.

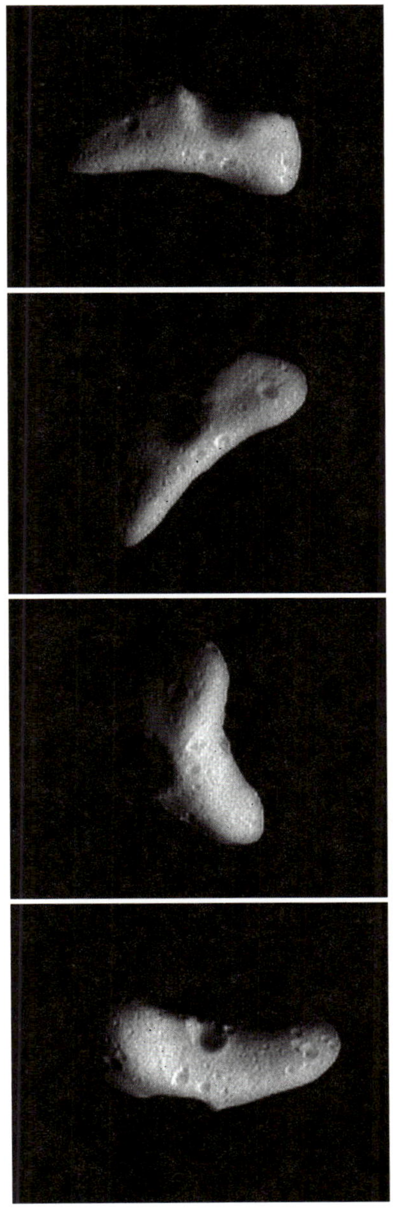

Figure 8.1 The rotation of Eros seen by the NEAR probe from a range of 1800 km above Eros's north pole, two days before NEAR entered orbit. The time between the first and last frame is 2 h 36 min.

TYP p. 99 mentions that an asteroid's rotation period can be deduced from periodic variations in its apparent brightness (i.e. in the amount sunlight reflected from it, which we can measure even when the body is too distant for its shape to be discernable through the most powerful telescope). This is because the asteroid's irregular shape means that the size of the visible sunlit area changes with the body's rotation. Imagine watching the rotation in Figure 8.1 from a viewpoint to the right: you would see the greatest area at the time of the third frame and the least area at the time of the first and fourth frames (when you would see the body end-on). An example of a graph of variation in apparent brightness, known as a 'light curve', is shown in Figure 8.2.

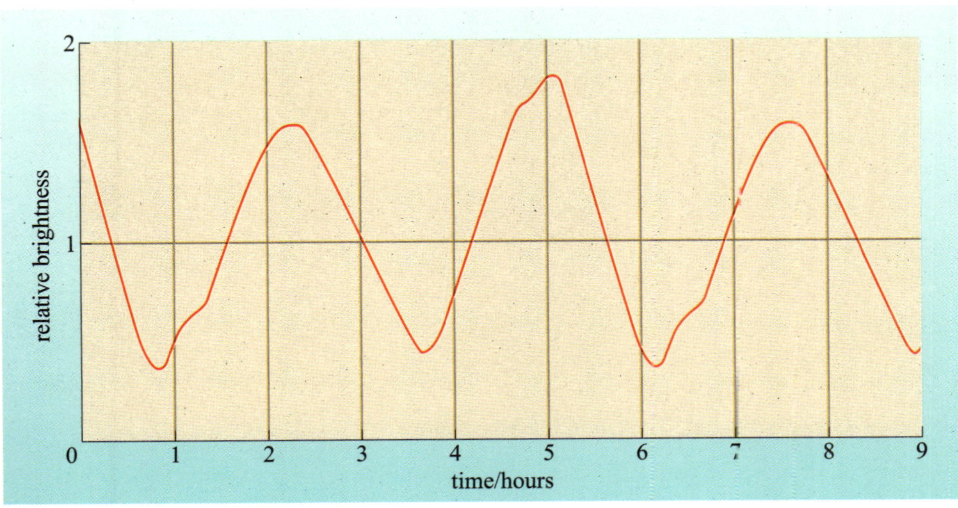

Figure 8.2 A light curve showing changes in apparent brightness of the asteroid Eros over time.

You should be able to discern in Figure 8.2 a repeating pattern in the apparent brightness of Eros as it rotates.

- On the basis of Figure 8.2, how long must it take for Eros to make a complete rotation?

- There are four minima in the apparent brightness during the interval recorded in the figure. A minimum must occur when Eros is seen as close to end-on as it gets from our viewpoint. On the other hand, the brightness must peak when we see the fullest view of a long face of the body. Starting from the minimum at 0 h 50 min on the light curve, the next minimum occurs at about 3 h 40 min. This represents about *half* a rotation, not a complete rotation, because we are now seeing the opposite end of the body to the one we saw at 0 h 50 min. A complete rotation has occurred when we reach the next minimum, at about 6 h 10 min. The complete rotation thus took from about 0 h 50 min until about 6 h 10 min, which is a duration of about 5 h 20 min (5.33 hours).

You would get the same period by measuring the time between the matching peaks at 2 h 20 min and 7 h 40 min. The accepted value for Eros's rotation period of 5.27 hours (*TYP* Table 8.1) is more accurate, because it was derived by observing over a longer period and dividing the total time by a large number of rotations.

8.1.2 Asteroid names and provisional designations

TYP pp. 99–100 describe provisional designations for newly discovered Solar System bodies, which they bear instead of names until sufficient observations have been accumulated to determine their orbits properly. The same provisional designation system is shared by asteroids and Kuiper belt objects. A simpler system is used for suspected new satellites of planets, which will become apparent when you see the tables that list new satellites in Chapters 9–11.

On *TYP* p. 100, 905th is a misprint for 906th.

TYP p. 100 gives the example of 1998 SF_{36}. This provisional designation indicates the 906th object discovered in the period 16–30 September of 1998. The rules indicated in Table 8.1 show how this works. The *first* letter, in this case S, simply indicates the period 16–30 September. The body with provisional designation 1998 SF would be the sixth body discovered in that period, the *second* letter in the designation, F, being the sixth letter of the alphabet. 1998 SZ would be the 25th, Z being the 25th letter given that I is not used. The 26th discovery in this period would be 1998 SA_1, in which A_1 indicates 1 + 25, and the 27th would be 1998 SB_1, in which B_1 indicates 2 + 25. 1998 SA_2 would be the 51st discovery in the period, in which A_2 indicates $1 + (2 \times 25)$. So in 1998 SF_{36}, F_{36} indicates $6 + (36 \times 25)$, which is 906.

Question 8.2

Following the same principles, work out as fully as possible when the following objects were discovered: (a) 1994 XM_1; (b) 2000 WO_{107}. ◀

Table 8.1 Letter codes for provisional designation of newly discovered asteroids and other minor planets.

The half-month of discovery is given by the *first* letter in the designation (I and Z are not used):

Letter	Dates	Letter	Dates
A	1–15 January	B	16–31 January
C	1–15 February	D	16–29 February
E	1–15 March	F	16–31 March
G	1–15 April	H	16–30 April
J	1–15 May	K	16–31 May
L	1–15 June	M	16–30 June
N	1–15 July	O	16–31 July
P	1–15 August	Q	16–31 August
R	1–15 September	S	16–30 September
T	1–15 October	U	16–31 October
V	1–15 November	W	16–30 November
X	1–15 December	Y	16–31 December

The order of discovery within the half-month, is given by the *second* letter in the designation (I is not used):

1 = A, 2 = B, 3 = C, 4 = D, 5 = E, 6 = F, 7 = G, 8 = H, 9 = J, 10 = K,
11 = L, 12 = M, 13 = N, 14 = O, 15 = P, 16 = Q, 17 = R, 18 = S,
19 = T, 20 = U, 21 = V, 22 = W, 23 = X, 24 = Y, 25 = Z.

The next 25 discoveries in the half-month repeat the same two-letter designation series, followed by a subscript 1, the next 25 repeat it again followed by a subscript 2, and so on.

8.1.3 The rest of Chapter 8

The remainder of *TYP* Chapter 8 is one of the parts of book that was most heavily revised between the original (2000) edition and the new (2003) edition that you are using for this course. This is thanks largely to advances in understanding gained through intensive telescopic surveys, driven primarily by concerns over asteroids able to collide with the Earth. Additionally, a large database of information was accumulated for Eros by the NEAR mission. A library of asteroid images from spacecraft and telescopes is included on the S196 CD-ROM.

There are just a few additional comments to make:

- The surface of every asteroid imaged by a passing spacecraft has turned out to be fairly densely cratered. This was no surprise. As expected in view of the unique collision history of each object, the abundance and proportions of craters of different sizes vary from object to object. However, the especially detailed images of Eros obtained by NEAR revealed a puzzling lack of craters less than a few tens of metres in diameter, particularly in certain areas. Instead, much of Eros has an abundance of boulders a few metres across with the notable exception of some smooth (dust-filled?) hollows (Figure 8.3).

Figure 8.3 A NEAR close-up image of a 340 m wide area of Eros. This area is densely strewn with boulders, except for the much smoother area in the upper left.

- Hubble Space Telescope images of Vesta, the third-largest asteroid, revealing dark (presumably basalt) patches on its surface (*TYP* p. 102) and also its non-spherical shape, are shown on the S196 CD-ROM under 'Other Asteroids' as Asteroid2 and 3.
- *TYP* p. 102 includes the first mention of a category of tarry substances called tholins. Tholins crop up in subsequent chapters as likely ingredients of the surface materials on many of the satellites of the outer planets and Kuiper belt objects.

- Images of asteroids with satellites are shown in Figure 8.4. You will find a movie version of the top component of this Figure on the S196 CD-ROM under 'Other Asteroids' as Asteroid8.
- You may have found it hard to fathom the statement on *TYP* p. 105 that you are just as likely to be killed by an asteroid impact as in a plane crash. If so, consider this. A plane crash is likely to kill at most hundreds of people. A large asteroid impact could kill hundreds of millions in one go. Thus although asteroid impacts are very much rarer than plane crashes, the average death-rates are similar when averaged out over a sufficiently long duration. Asteroids and comets whose orbits frequently carry them close to the Earth, and which could therefore potentially hit the Earth, are collectively described as Near-Earth Objects (NEOs). If you have Internet access you can find out more about these objects and current efforts to catalogue and characterize them via http://neo.jpl.nasa.gov.

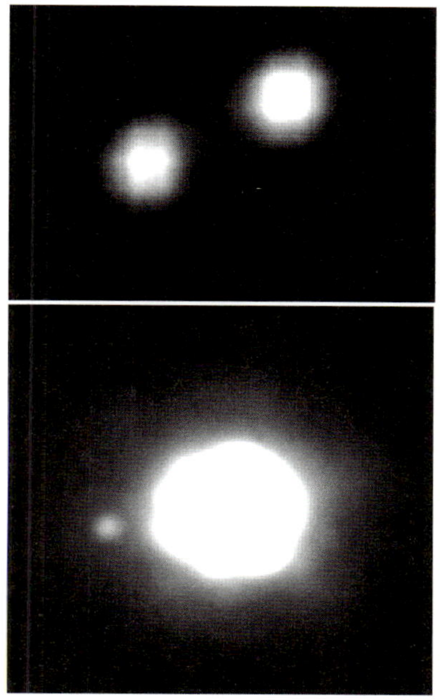

Figure 8.4 Top: The double asteroid Antiope, as imaged using the adaptive optics of the Keck telescope in Hawaii. Bottom: Pulcova (140 km diameter) and its 15 km diameter satellite, seen using the Canada-France-Hawaii telescope. (Images courtesy of NASA and Southwest Research Institute).

8.2 Chapter 8 questions

Now try to answer the following questions, to remind you of some of the things you have learned and test your understanding of them.

Question 8.3

What are the simplest reasons for not counting any of the asteroids as a planet? ◀

Question 8.4

Which statement about asteroids in the list is correct?

A Although covered by regolith, they are mostly solid rock.

B Asteroid composition bears no relationship to orbital period.

C Asteroids with satellites are extremely rare.

D Very few asteroids have an orbital period close to 5.93 years.

E Many asteroids have retrograde orbits. ◀

Question 8.5

What will be the provisional designation of the 210th minor planet discovered in the second half of March 2010? ◀

Question 8.6

The asteroid Eugenia orbits the Sun at an average distance of 2.78 AU. What is its orbital period? (Use Equation 2.1 and the method of Question 2.6 to calculate your answer). ◀

9 Jupiter

Now study *TYP* Chapter 9. This is the longest chapter in the book, partly because Jupiter is the first of the giant planets and partly because it has a large family of satellites. Four of these are much more substantial than any asteroid and can justifiably be regarded as worlds in their own rights. You may find it useful to break this potentially long period of study by returning here for a discussion of Jupiter itself before you begin to read about rings and satellites (*TYP* p. 119). If you prefer to carry on through to the end of the chapter first that's fine too.

9.1 Discussion of Chapter 9

9.1.1 Jupiter itself

Figure 9.1 A Hubble Space Telescope image of Jupiter, showing the complete sunlit hemisphere as it appeared on 5 October 1995. The arrow indicates the site where the Galileo entry probe descended below the cloud tops 63 days later.

TYP p. 105 describes Jupiter's visibly flattened shape as a result of the planet's rapid rotation. The flattening is not really apparent in *TYP* Figure 9.1, because the terminator (the day-night boundary) is within the left-hand edge of the visible half of the globe. The flattened shape is better seen in Figure 9.1 here, in which the sunlit hemisphere is seen full-on.

TYP Table 9.1 lists a future mission named Europa Orbiter. Unfortunately, this has since been cancelled, but instead NASA now proposes a highly ambitious mission provisionally called Jupiter Icy Moons Orbiter for launch in 2011 at the earliest. If you have Internet access and want to keep track of plans as they evolve, you can do so by selecting the Jupiter option at http://sse.jpl.nasa.gov/missions, and then selecting the 'future' option.

TYP p. 111 mentions the onward journeys of the two Voyager spacecraft towards interstellar space. By January 2003, Voyager 1 had reached over 87 AU from the Sun and Voyager 2 over 69 AU. Both spacecraft were healthy, with enough power to keep them operational until at least 2020.

TYP p. 113 describes Jupiter's enormously strong magnetic field, and p. 110 mentions the associated radiation belt of magnetically-confined charged particles that are liable to damage the electronics of any spacecraft that lingers too long. Figure 9.2 shows views of the inner and most intense part of the radiation zone. Another version is on the S196 CD-ROM as Jupiter7, and Jupiter6 shows a greater extent of the radiation zone detected by a different method. A colour version of *TYP* Figure 9.3 showing an aurora where the magnetic field channels charged particles into the atmosphere appears as Jupiter4, and a more powerful and spectacular aurora recorded in the ultraviolet is shown in Jupiter5.

Figure 9.2 Two views of Jupiter recorded about half a rotation (5 hours) apart by Cassini, a Saturn-bound mission that flew past Jupiter at the start of 2001. The planet is seen in visible light, but the colourful patches on either side indicate the intensity of radiation mapped by a detector of microwaves.

The strong radiation zone in Figure 9.2 is actually hoop-like in shape, and runs right round the planet. However, the figure makes it look like separate patches to either side of the globe because this is where our line of sight passes through the greatest extent of the zone. To visualize this, imagine sticking a knitting needle into a ring doughnut: a needle pointing towards the centre would only pass through a couple of centimetres before reaching the hole, whereas a needle parallel to this but off to the side would miss the hole and pass through a lot more cake before emerging again.

Bearing in mind information given in *The interior* (*TYP* pp. 112–114), why do you think the location of the radiation belt relative to the planet appears to change between the two images in Figure 9.2?

The two images were obtained half a rotation apart, and the 'wobble' in the orientation of the radiation belt arises because the axis of the magnetic field is tilted relative to Jupiter's rotation axis (by nearly 10° according to *TYP* p. 113).

The circulation of Jupiter's atmosphere is discussed in *The atmosphere* (*TYP* pp. 114–117), and the movies Jupiter21-27 on the S196 CD-ROM document various scales of atmospheric motion, including rotation of the Great Red Spot. The clouds forming the opaque 'surface' to Jupiter's atmosphere are presumed to be created by ammonia (NH_3) condensing out of a vapour to form tiny suspended crystals of ammonia ice.

In what way does the composition of Jupiter's clouds differ from those in the Earth's atmosphere?

Clouds on Earth are made of water; usually in the form of tiny liquid droplets, but sometimes as ice crystals, especially for the highest clouds (see Section 5.1.2). Jupiter's topmost clouds have a different composition (ammonia), and are tiny crystals rather than liquid droplets. The same goes for Jupiter's next layer of cloud below the visible one, which is of ammonium hydrosulfide, but there is believed to be a (hitherto unproven) third layer of cloud made of water ice crystals below this (*TYP* p. 117).

Jupiter's topmost cloud layer does not mark the top of the atmosphere, which continues for some hundreds of kilometres above the cloud deck, becoming ever more tenuous with altitude. The traditional interpretation of Jupiter's Hadley circulation (illustrated here in Figure 9.3 and described on *TYP* p. 116) is that the atmosphere rises in the zones and sinks in the intervening belts (which appear darker because the cloud tops are seen through a greater depth of atmosphere). However, thorough analysis of Jupiter images recorded between October 2000 and March 2001 by the Saturn-bound Cassini mission (*TYP* Table 9.1) suggests that, on the contrary, the belts are where the atmosphere rises.

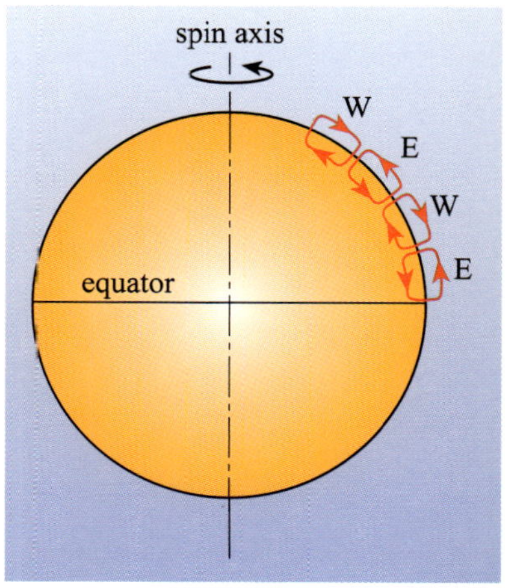

Figure 9.3 The traditional view of Hadley cells in Jupiter's atmosphere. E means that there is flow to the east, and W to the west.

See Box 9.1 for the story as released by NASA to the press in March 2003 (too late to be incorporated in *TYP*). You will be expected to understand what is said in press releases like this and in similar stories as retold by the news media in order to answer some of the questions in Chapters 12 and 14 and in the End of Course Assessment.

Box 9.1 NASA Press Release

Rising Storms Revise Story of Jupiter's Stripes – March 6, 2003

Pictures of Jupiter, taken by a NASA spacecraft on its way to Saturn, are flipping at least one long-standing notion about Jupiter upside down.

Stripes dominate Jupiter's appearance. Darker 'belts' alternate with lighter 'zones'. Scientists have long considered the zones, with their pale clouds, to be areas of upwelling atmosphere, partly because many clouds on Earth form where air is rising. On the principle of what goes up must come down, the dark belts have been viewed as areas where air generally descends.

However, pictures from the Cassini spacecraft show that individual storm cells of upwelling bright-white clouds, too small to see from Earth, pop up almost without exception in the dark belts. Earlier spacecraft had hinted so, but not with the overwhelming evidence provided by the new images of 43 different storms.

'We have a clear picture emerging that the belts must be the areas of net-rising atmospheric motion on Jupiter, with the implication that the net motion in the zones has to be sinking,' said Dr Tony Del Genio, an atmospheric scientist at NASA's Goddard Institute for Space Studies, New York. 'It's the opposite of expectations for the past 50 years,' he said.

Del Genio is one of 24 co-authors from America and Europe reporting diverse results from the Cassini imaging of Jupiter in Friday's edition of the journal Science. Cassini's camera took about 26,000 images of Jupiter, its moons and its faint rings over a six-month period as the spacecraft passed nearby two years ago.

In fact, no one has actually measured Jupiter's atmosphere rising or sinking. The new theory announced in 2003 merely *infers* that the atmosphere in the belts is rising because the 'small' bright clouds within the belts that are referred to in the press release seem to indicate storm turbulence of a kind that ought to occur only during uprise, but not during sinking. Only time will tell whether this radically new interpretation of Jupiter's atmosphere becomes accepted. This is a timely reminder that little in planetary science is known with absolute certainty. Many mysteries remain, ranging from the apparently trivial, such as the scarcity of very small craters on Eros (Section 8.1.3), to the fundamental, such as this example of how the atmosphere of the biggest planet circulates.

The successive collisions of fragments of comet Shoemaker Levy 9 onto Jupiter captivated the world's media in July 1994, and you may remember these events yourself. A view of the tidally disrupted comet six months before the collision is shown in Figure 9.4 and movies of two of the collisions appear on the S196 CD-ROM as Jupiter28 and29.

Try the following questions to help to test your understanding of Jupiter's atmosphere and interior before continuing with the rest of the chapter.

Question 9.1

(a) How does Jupiter's Hadley circulation differ from that in the atmospheres of the terrestrial planets, and what might be the main reasons for the differences? (For the purposes of this answer, you can assume that the 'traditional' interpretation of Jupiter's atmosphere is correct.)

(b) What other factors distinguish Jupiter's atmosphere from these others? ◀

Figure 9.4 Hubble Space Telescope view of the strung-out fragments of comet Shoemaker Levy 9 on 24 January 1994.

Question 9.2

What are the composition and physical state of Jupiter's interior thought to be at a depth of about 12 000 km? ◀

If you have not already done so, you should now study the remainder of Chapter 9 (*TYP* pp. 119–139). Return here when you have finished.

9.1.2 Rings and the satellite family

There can be few people who have never heard of the rings of Saturn, but you may have been surprised to discover in this course that every one of the giant planets has rings, including Jupiter. Another feature common to the giant planets is that each has a numerous family of satellites. The likeness goes deeper than that, because there are strong similarities in the organization of each of these families. There are small inner satellites ('moonlets') in near-circular prograde orbits that lie virtually in the plane of the planet's equator, some of which are intimately associated with the ring system. Farther out come the 'regular satellites', which are the only ones large enough to have taken on spherical shapes, and except at Neptune these are also in low-inclination near-circular prograde orbits. There are four of these at Jupiter, which are the ones discovered by Galileo Galilei in 1610 (Figure 1.3) and collectively referred to as the galilean satellites. Beyond these are smaller 'irregular satellites' in less circular and more strongly inclined orbits, which are commonly retrograde.

Generally speaking, the outer satellites are thought to have originated as asteroids, comet nuclei or Kuiper belt objects that strayed close enough to the planet to become captured. In contrast, the large prograde satellites grew in association with their planet from a circumplanetary disc of gas and dust, as described on *TYP* p. 17. The small inner satellites are probably remnants of larger satellites that were destroyed by collision or came within the planet's Roche limit and were ripped apart by tides. The same processes could account for some of the ring material too.

Twenty-two outer satellites of Jupiter were identified in the period 1999-2001, and many of these are still denoted by provisional designations in *TYP* Table 9.2. These were all telescopic discoveries, and the discovery images (i.e. the images on which the object was discovered) of one of them are shown in Figure 9.5. The provisional designation system for satellites is simpler than that for minor planets, as you can deduce from the examples in the table. They begin with S (to signify a presumed satellite) followed by the year of discovery. Next comes a letter to indicate the planet (J for Jupiter, S for Saturn, U for Uranus) followed by a number to indicate the order of discovery for that planet in that year. Only one discovery from the year 2000 still bears its provisional designation in the table, all the others having been awarded names in October 2002.

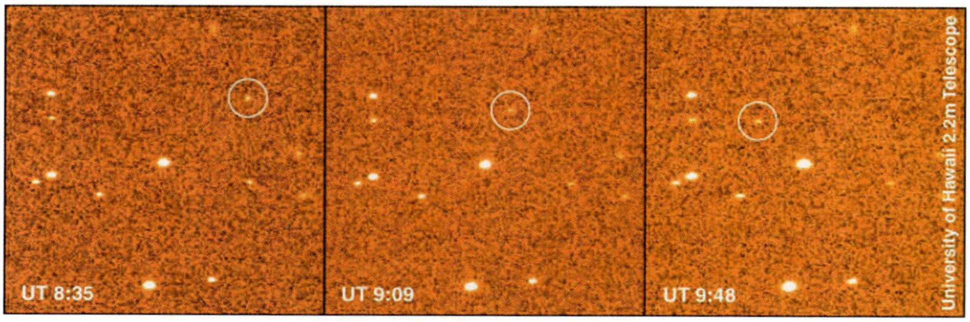

Figure 9.5 The discovery images of S2000 J8 (which was awarded the name Magaclite in October 2002), made on 5 December 2000 by the University of Hawaii 2.2 m telescope. Three images are shown, covering a 71 minute period. The satellite (with a circle put round it to help you see it) clearly moves relative to the background stars.

Too late for inclusion in your edition of *TYP*, telescopic discoveries of a further 20 retrograde and one prograde irregular outer satellites of Jupiter were announced in March–May 2003 (you can find out more at http://www.ifa.hawaii.edu/~sheppard/satellites/jup2003.html).

- What provisional designations will have been allotted to these bodies?
- The first was designated S/2003 J1, the second was S/2003 J2, and so on up to S/2003 J21.

None of these exceeds about 4 km in size. The innermost of the 20 new retrograde satellites (S/2003 J3) has an orbit about a million kilometres within that of S/2001 J10, and the outermost (S/2003/J2) holds the current record as the outermost of Jupiter's entire family at 28.6 million km. S/2003 J20 became the outermost known prograde satellite, with an orbital radius of about 17 million km.

Note that these discoveries increase the total of Jupiter's known satellites to 61. You may like to reflect this by correcting the total in the Jupiter *Planetary facts* table on *TYP* p. 108. However, use pencil rather than ink, because the number will go down if any of the new discoveries is discredited or, more likely, increase as additional discoveries are announced.

- What do you think had happened that allowed the year 2000 discoveries other than S/2000 J11 to receive official names by the time *TYP* Table 9.2 was prepared?
- A sufficient number of observations had been made for their orbital motion about Jupiter to be adequately determined. This is the same principle as applied to the awarding of names to minor planets. Also, appropriate names (usually suggested by the discoverers) had been agreed by a committee of the IAU.

All the names of Jupiter's longer-known satellites are of characters associated with Jupiter, or his equivalent Zeus, in Greco-Roman mythology. The IAU has continued this theme for the new discoveries, with the refinement among the outer satellites that those in prograde orbits have been given mainly Latin names ending in -a whereas those in retrograde orbits have been given mainly Greek names ending in -e. Figure 9.6 illustrates the general disposition of the outer satellite orbits.

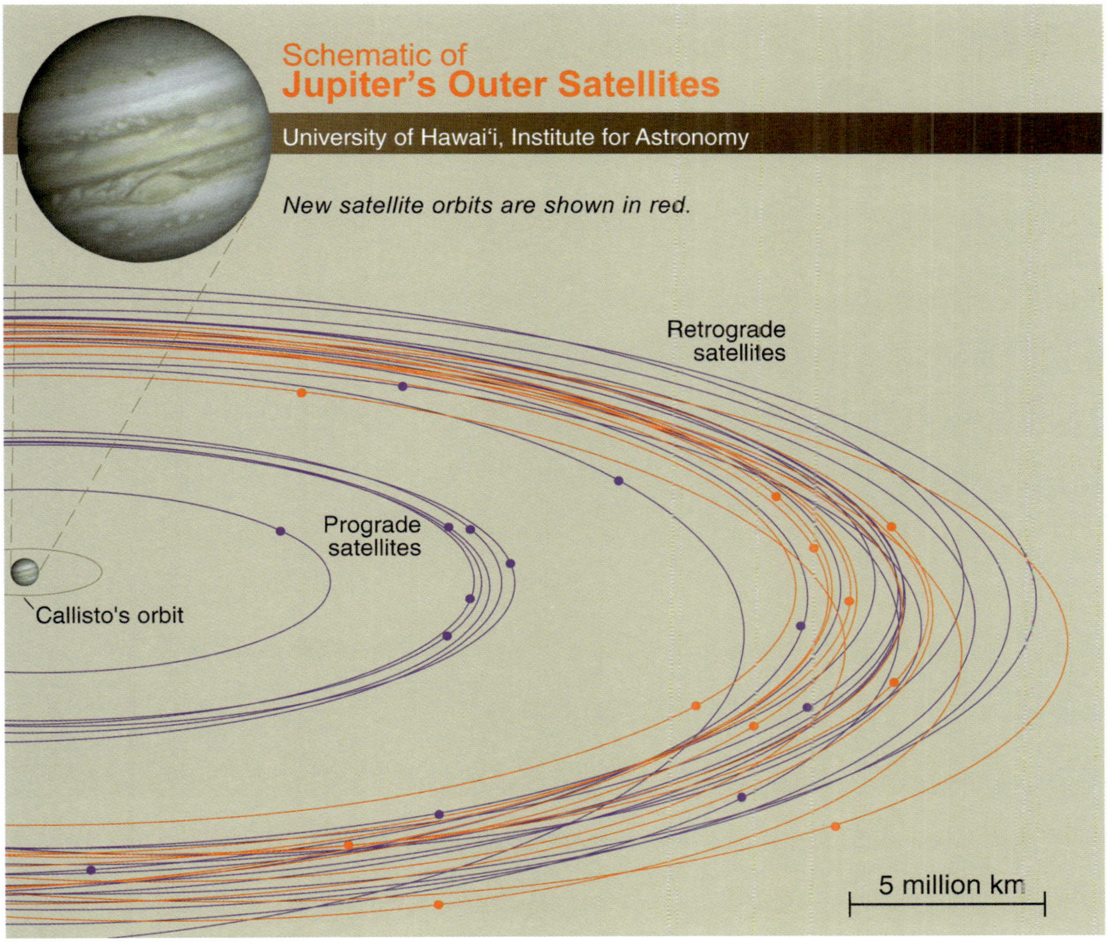

Figure 9.6 A perspective diagram of Jupiter's satellite system, showing all orbits from Callisto (the outermost galilean satellite) outwards. The orbits of 2001 discoveries are distinguished in red. Discoveries announced after the end of 2002 are not included. (University of Hawaii and Scott Sheppard/David Jewitt)

We probably now know more about each of the galilean satellites than we do about Mercury. Their diverse properties and large size fully justify treating them individually in a course about planets.

9.1.3 Io

Io is one of the most marvellous bodies in the Solar System, but the intense radiation bathing its surface (Figure 9.2) makes it unlikely that anyone will ever be able to visit. Even robotic spacecraft cannot survive this close to Jupiter for very long, so the Galileo Jupiter orbiter made very few close fly-bys of Io. However, there is by now a remarkable collection of images from close fly-bys and farther away, represented in *TYP* by Plate 8 and Figures 9.10–9.12 and the additional Io images on the S196 CD-ROM.

One of the most spectacular Galileo images of Io is reproduced in Figure 9.7. On this image the orange glow of the incandescent lava is genuine. It was recorded in visible light, and represents pretty much what you could have seen with your own eyes (before you were killed by the radiation!). This contrasts with most other images of active lava flows on Io such as Io12-16, 20 and 23 on the S196 CD-ROM, on which the hot areas were detected using infrared radiation, but were not necessarily hot enough or powerful enough to generate a detectable glow in the visible part of the spectrum. On those false-colour images (Box 3.3), the infrared signal is displayed in red.

Figure 9.7 Io seen in visible light during a close-pass by Galileo on 29 November 1999. Most of the red-hot area is a 10 km high curtain of incandescent lava fragments erupting from a 100 km long fissure. A short glowing lava flow can also be seen. The image is 800 km across.

Most of the names on Io are taken from gods and heroes associated with fire, thunder or the Sun, or from Dante's *Inferno*. Eruptive centres on Io share with impact craters the distinction of being the only features whose names are not qualified by a descriptor term. Thus Prometheus (Plate 8), Zanama (*TYP* Figure 9.11) and Pele (*TYP* Figure 9.12) are complete names with nothing missing. However, a few eruptive centres identified by some kind of topographic attribute do take descriptor terms, one example being Pillan Patera in Plate 8 and *TYP* Figure 9.12. The fissure-shaped vent in Figure 9.7 has not been named, but the larger feature in which it occurs is called Tvashtar Catena.

- Refer back to Table 2.1. What does 'Catena' mean?
- This is a descriptor term signifying a chain of craters. In this case it is evidently a chain of volcanic depressions (which a geologist would call 'calderas') rather than a chain of impact craters. (Tvashtar, incidentally, is a Hindu Sun god and smith.)

The most important general point to learn from study of Io is that it demonstrates how tidal heating can add enormously to the supply of heat leaking towards the surface of a planetary body. Tidal heating was introduced on *TYP* p. 21. It operates among the inner three galilean satellites because they are in orbital resonance (with a ratio between their periods of 1 : 2 : 4). The details of how orbital resonance leads to tidal heating are beyond this course. All you need to know is that it is to do with the regularly repeated gravitational tugs between satellites as they pass and the extent to which this prevents the tidal drag of the planet from forcing the satellite's orbits to become circular. [See Box 9.2 for a further clarification about orbital resonance.]

Box 9.2 Orbital resonance: further clarification

When it comes to causing tidal heating, the ratio between the orbital periods of two satellites has to be much closer to a simple ratio than in the asteroid examples discussed in Box 8.1, where the issue was the extent to which their orbits round the Sun were controlled by interplay with Jupiter. For tidal heating purposes, two satellites of a large planet having a ratio between their orbital periods of 2.1 : 1 certainly will not experience tidal heating, because this ratio is too different from exactly 2 : 1. However, 2.01 : 1 or 1.99 : 1 would probably be close enough.

9.1.4 Europa

Although Io may be more spectacular, Europa is perhaps more intriguing. To get the most out of this section you needed to look more carefully at images in *TYP* (such as *TYP* Figures 9.14 and 9.15 and Plate 9) than was necessary earlier in the course. This is because even though Europa's landscape is so alien, the images contain clues as to the processes that have shaped it. Many of the Europa images on the S196 CD-ROM will repay study too, in particular Europa16, which shows the larger region surrounding *TYP* Figure 9.14 and Plate 9. Part of this is shown here as Figure 9.8. You may find it particularly illuminating to go to Europa16 and click within any of the three outlined areas to call up a higher resolution image of that local area. You can then use your browser's 'back' and 'forward' buttons to 'toggle' between the local and regional views.

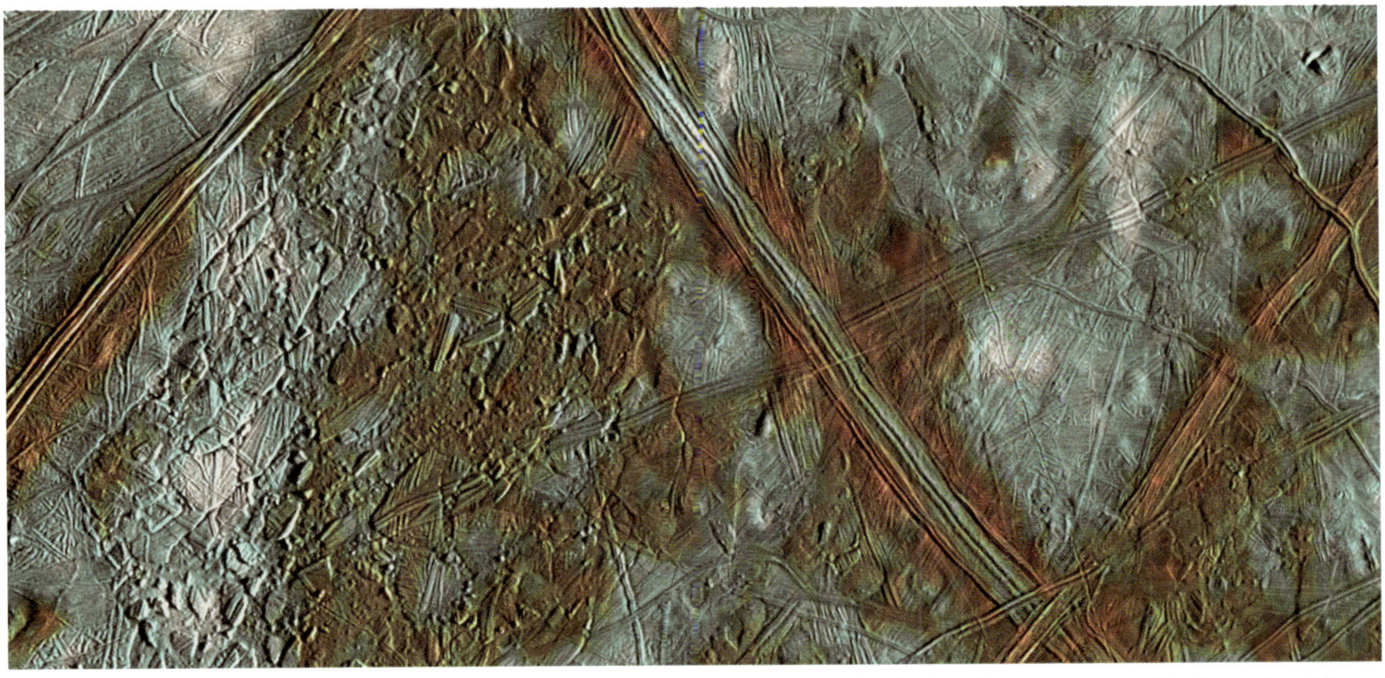

Figure 9.8 A 200 km wide area of Europa, illuminated from the right. 'Ball-of-string' surface patterns predominate, but this surface pattern has been disrupted in several places, notably in Conamara Chaos on the left, which is shown in a more detailed image in *TYP* Plate 9. The colours are exaggerated. The reddest areas are probably the saltiest, purer ice appears blue, and white patches are powdery ejecta from a distant impact crater. The area shown here is extracted from S196 CD-ROM Europa 16.

Question 9.3

Look carefully at the area shown in Figure 9.8 and see if you can use your logic to put the following events into the correct time sequence within this area, starting with the oldest first: (a) disruption of surface by breakup into chaos, (b) generation of ball-of-string surface (refer to *TYP* Figure 9.14 for a good example of ball-of-string surface), (c) formation of ridge systems larger in scale than the typical ball-of-string texture, (d) patchy distribution of white ejecta. You may find it helpful toggle between Europa16 and Europa10 on the S196 CD-ROM. *This is a challenging question – if you are really stuck then study the answer carefully, because this should make similar tasks easier for you in future. However, please have a go first – working this out does not depend on any skills specific to planetary science, instead it is a matter of logic and common sense.* ◀

TYP pp. 130–131 introduce the properties of Solar System ice that enable it to behave so much like rock, and the strange term 'cryovolcanism' that you will meet in connection with several other icy satellites. Europa is atypical because the ice (being so thin and warm at its base) can sometimes behave rather like frozen sea-ice on Earth, but on the other icy satellites of the outer planets the likenesses to silicate rock in a terrestrial planet are much stronger.

The Europa section concludes (*TYP* pp. 132–133) with speculation about the possibility of life nourished by chemical energy beside hot springs on the floor of Europa's ocean. This is the kind of setting where it is now believed that life is most likely to have begun on the Earth. However, you should bear in mind that there is no proof that Europa's ocean exists, although at present that does seem to be the simplest way to explain the drifted rafts in some of the chaos regions. Now that NASA's Europa Orbiter has been cancelled (Section 9.1.1), the responsibility of verifying the existence of its ocean will fall to the Jupiter Icy Moons Orbiter.

9.1.5 Ganymede and Callisto

The images of Ganymede and Callisto in *TYP* and the others on the S196 CD-ROM demonstrate that ancient icy surfaces can display just as large a range of features as any rocky world. Given the similarity in properties between ice and rock listed on *TYP* p. 130, this should not be surprising. For example, most impact craters on Callisto and the younger impact craters on Ganymede (Figure 9.9) look pretty much the same as impact craters on Mercury, the Moon or Mars. Similarly, Callisto's Valhalla impact basin (*TYP* Figure 9.18) resembles multiringed impact basins of terrestrial planets such as Mercury's Caloris basin (*TYP* Figure 3.2).

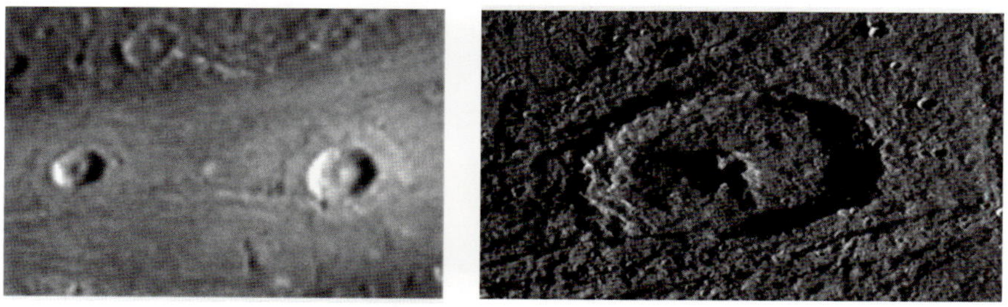

Figure 9.9 Left: relatively young craters on Ganymede, the largest having a well-formed central peak. This is an enlarged extract of part of *TYP* Figure 9.17. Right: a higher resolution view of a similar crater on Ganymede, 32 km in diameter.

- From which direction is the illumination coming in each of the images in Figure 9.9?

- The shadows on the crater floors cast by the walls and central peaks demonstrate that the illumination is from the right in both cases.

The only important distinction between cratering on the terrestrial planets and on Jupiter's satellites concerns the *rate* of cratering. There is clear evidence from the relative abundances of craters of different sizes that the population of impactors responsible for craters on Ganymede and Callisto differs from the population that caused the cratering of the terrestrial planets. The reason is that the latter is probably dominated by asteroids, whereas the former may include a greater proportion of comets plus locally generated debris arising from collisions within the particular satellite system. Whatever the explanation, it means that (as you may remember from Section 2.2.2) we cannot use the lunar cratering time-scale to determine the absolute ages of the surfaces of the galilean satellites. Even more frustrating is that the impactor populations at Saturn, Uranus and Neptune all seem to have been different, so that we cannot use craters to compare ages between satellite systems in the outer Solar System. All that it is usually safe to assume is that when comparing regions on the same body, a more densely cratered surface must be older than a less densely cratered surface.

The surfaces of Ganymede and Callisto are much older than any surface that has survived on Europa, and this is where you first meet the concept of icy surfaces becoming darker as they age. This is a principle that seems to apply pretty well among the satellites of the outer planets. Age-darkening is a combination of two processes. One is the gradual concentration of residual rocky or sooty (carbonaceous) particles as the ice is removed by molecules being broken apart by radiation (water ice, for example, gets split into hydrogen and oxygen) or vaporized in small meteorite impact events. The other is loss of oxygen or hydrogen from carbon-bearing ice molecules (such as carbon dioxide, CO_2, or methane, CH_4) to leave sooty carbon or tarry molecules known as tholins, which you met on *TYP* p. 102.

Age is not the only factor controlling the albedo of ice. Its physical state is important too. If you make a powder out of anything solid, the powder will probably be paler than what you started with. This is why young craters and their ejecta are usually such bright features, although these too darken with age. Age-darkening is too slow to have affected Europa's young surface, and here the contrast between pale and dark areas must be largely due to the texture of the ice. For example, in *TYP* Figure 9.13 the dark 'cracks' are clearly younger than the bright plains that they cut. Rather than being related to age, this contrast could reflect differences in the size of the ice crystals or the roughness of the surface.

Try to bear in mind when you compare images of different icy satellites that this will not usually tell you about their albedos, because the brightness of each image will usually have been adjusted to show each body to the best advantage. For example, in *TYP* Figure 9.16 Callisto has been brightened relative to Ganymede so that features in each one show up well. With an average albedo of 0.7, Europa is more than three times as reflective as Callisto, whose albedo is only 0.2. Figure 9.10 here shows the true relative brightnesses of the three icy galilean satellites.

Figure 9.10 Europa, Ganymede and Callisto shown at their correct relative sizes and their correct relative brightnesses. In this rendering, the image of Europa is rather too bleached out to show its features well, whereas Callisto is very dark except for its more recent impact craters.

You should not come away from this chapter with the impression that the galilean satellites are well understood. For example, the great abundance of craters on Callisto suggests an ancient surface, and the absence of fractures or cryovolcanic features suggests that its outer shell (which would equate with the lithosphere of a terrestrial planet) must be very thick. However, Callisto's magnetic field suggests a salty ocean no more than 100 km below the surface. It is hard to see how both can be right. I am inclined to suspect that the magnetic data collected by Galileo have been misinterpreted, and that Callisto has no ocean, or at least not at such a shallow depth – but I could be wrong.

9.2 Chapter 9 questions

Now try to answer the following questions, to remind you of some of the things you have learned and test your understanding of them.

Question 9.4

To the nearest order of magnitude, how much greater is the estimated rate of heat loss per square metre of surface on Io than on Earth? ◀

Question 9.5

From the list, which is the correct reason why Io is so volcanically active?

A Io orbits within a strong, magnetically confined, belt of radiation.

B Io is tidally heated.

C Io contains an anomalously high concentration of radioactive elements.

D A lot of primordial heat is still leaking away on Io. ◀

Question 9.6

Apart from the fact that they orbit Jupiter rather than the Sun, do (a) Io and (b) Europa lack any properties that would otherwise allow them to be regarded as terrestrial planets? ◀

Question 9.7

From the list, which of the following is not likely to happen to molecules of water on Europa or Ganymede?

A Radiation can break them down into oxygen and hydrogen.

B Radiation can turn them into tholins.

C They can react with chemicals in rock.

D They can become components in cryovolcanic fluids. ◀

Question 9.8

Look at the image in Figure 9.11. This is part of a map of one of the galilean satellites derived from a mixture of Voyager and Galileo images and which shows some IAU-approved names. This extract covers 80° of longitude and nearly 60° of latitude.

(a) What are the features with one-word names, such as Dendera, Antum and Maa?

(b) What is the meaning of 'Sulcus' in two-word names such as Umma Sulcus and Nippur Sulcus?

(c) Which of the galilean satellites is this map from, and how can you tell? ◀

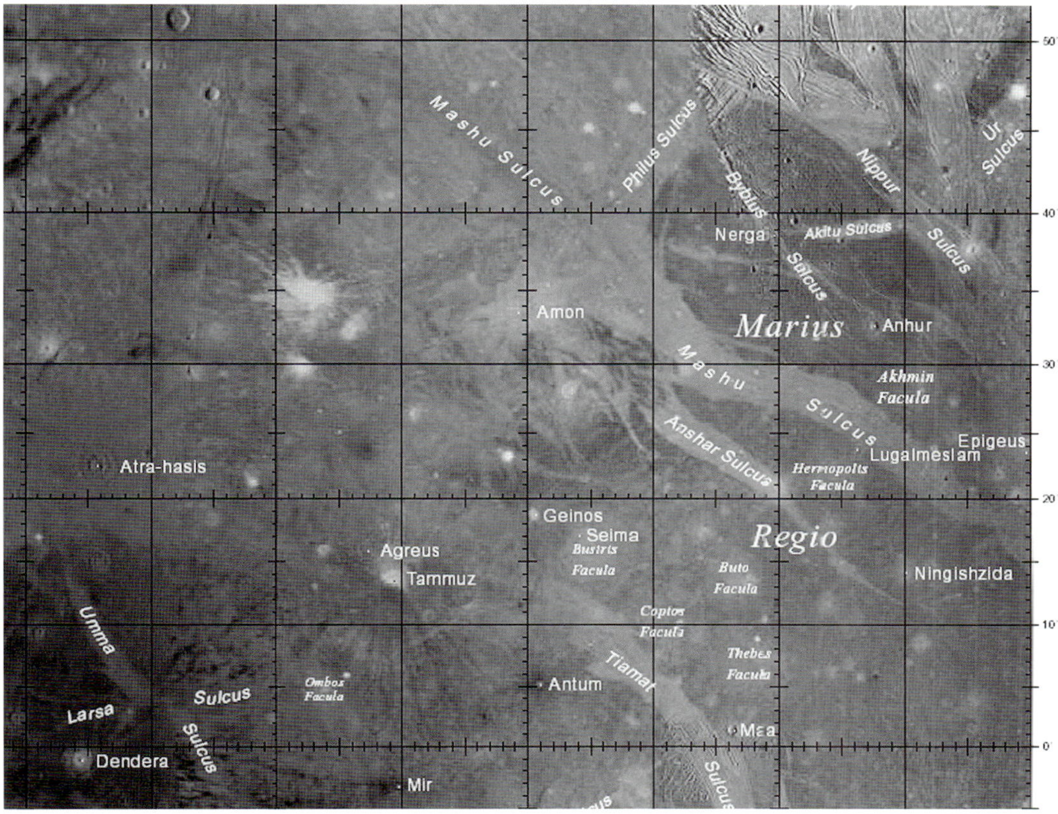

Figure 9.11 An image-based map showing part of one of the galilean satellites. For use with Question 9.8.

10 Saturn

Now study *TYP* Chapter 10. This is another long chapter, because Saturn has so many satellites worthy of discussion, even though only one ranks with the galilean satellites in terms of size. Return here when you have finished Chapter 10.

10.1 Discussion of Chapter 10

Please read the following discussion before attempting the questions in Section 10.2.

10.1.1 Saturn itself

It is not far wrong to regard Saturn as a smaller version of Jupiter. The main differences are:

- it lacks such a long-lived storm system as Jupiter's Great Red Spot (or, rather, it has done so during 300 years or so of telescopic scrutiny);
- because Saturn is less massive, its molecular hydrogen layer extends much deeper before the pressure is sufficient to compress it into metallic hydrogen (*TYP* Figure 2.5).

TYP p. 141 describes how Saturn's axial inclination causes the presentation of the rings to vary according to the planet's position round its orbit. This is shown by the rather pretty sequence of images in Figure 10.1.

There are several images of Saturn on the S196 CD-ROM that are worth looking at. In particular Saturn3 shows polar aurorae and Saturn8-10 illustrate atmospheric features, and are not repeated elsewhere in the course materials. Like Jupiter, Saturn's topmost cloud layer, which is all we ever see, is believed to consist of ammonia ice crystals. If you have Internet access and are studying this course in autumn 2004 or later, when the Cassini mission is expected to return images and other information from Saturn and its satellites, you will be able to keep abreast of new revelations at http://saturn.jpl.nasa.gov and http://ciclops.lpl.arizona.edu.

10.1.2 Rings and the satellite family

Saturn's rings are far more spectacular and complex than Jupiter's, and are easy to make out even with a small telescope. As the *TYP* p. 146 describes, there are two factors contributing to the prominence of Saturn's rings. One is that Saturn's ring material is metre-sized chunks of high-albedo ice, whereas Jupiter's rings are mostly low-albedo particles about a micrometre (a thousandth of a millimetre) in size. The other factor is that the total amount of material in Saturn's rings is very much greater than in Jupiter's. If you were to gather all Saturn's ring material together you could make a satellite about 100 km across. One estimate of the total mass in Saturn's rings is 10^{19} kg, and an estimate of the total mass in Jupiter's rings is 10^{13} kg.

- How many orders of magnitude more mass are there in Saturn's rings than in Jupiter's?

- To work this out you just have to divide one value by the other: $10^{19}\,\text{kg}/10^{13}\,\text{kg} = 10^{19}/10^{13} = 10^{19-13} = 10^{6}$, so Saturn's rings have six orders of magnitude more mass than Jupiter's. [Refer back to Box 6.1 if you had trouble with dividing the powers of ten to work this out.]

On this basis, Saturn's rings have about a million times more mass than Jupiter's. Actually, this could be a considerable underestimate of the difference, because some estimates of the mass of Jupiter's rings are as low as 10^8 kg. There are several images of Saturn's rings on the S196 CD-ROM. In particular you may like to inspect Saturn15 and 16, which show how the F ring changed from a twisted braid when Voyager 1 saw it in November 1980 to a featureless ribbon when Voyager 2 saw it in August 1981. Saturn15 also shows Prometheus, one of the 'shepherd' satellites that control the form and location of this ring.

Figure 10.1 A composite series of Hubble Space Telescope images of Saturn, documenting the changing orientation of the rings with respect to the Earth between 1996 (bottom) and 2000 (top).

Saturn's satellite family as listed in *TYP* Table 10.2 conforms pretty well to the general model given in the previous chapter (*TYP* p. 121). The inner 'moonlets' are those from Janus inwards, the 'regular satellites' are Mimas to Titan, and the 'irregular satellites' are Hyperion and beyond. Exceptions are three tiny 'Trojan' satellites (Calypso, Telesto and Helene), which are known to share orbits with two of the regular satellites (Tethys and Dione), and Iapetus (Figure 10.2), which although an irregular satellite in terms of its orbit (which has an inclination of 7.5°) is large enough to have taken on a spherical shape. A more minor difference is that Saturn has six regular satellites rather than Jupiter's four, but that only one of these, Titan, is as large as the galilean satellites. Phoebe, much the largest of the retrograde irregular satellites, will be the first object imaged in close-up when Cassini arrives in the Saturn system in November 2004, and this should be a great improvement on the best Voyager image (*TYP* Figure 10.7).

On 8 April 2003 (too late for inclusion in *TYP*) the IAU announced the telescopic discovery of an additional satellite of Saturn, increasing its known family to 31. This body was, of course, given the provisional designation S/2003 S1. Its mean distance from Saturn's centre is about 18 720 000 km, its radius is thought to be about 4 km, and it has an inclined retrograde orbit with a period of about 956 days.

Where would S/2003 S1 fit in an updated version of *TYP* Table 10.2, and what type of satellite is it?

Its orbit is such that it fits between S/2000 S9 and S/2000 S12, and it appears to be a perfectly ordinary irregular satellite.

If you have Internet access, you can read more about this discovery at http://www.ifa.hawaii.edu/~sheppard/satellites/sat2003.html.

10.1.3 Individual satellites

The rest of the chapter discusses each of the satellites large enough to be spherical, namely the regular satellites plus Iapetus. Here are some salient points:

Figure 10.2 The best Voyager colour image of Iapetus.

- The similarly sized neighbours Mimas and Enceladus are contrasted. Tidal heating has caused dramatic resurfacing of large parts of Enceladus, whereas there are no signs of this on Mimas.
- Tethys and Dione form another size pair. Both shows signs of having been partly resurfaced in the distant past, though each in a different style to Enceladus. An enlarged view of an old crater on Tethys that only just escaped obliteration by cryovolcanic flooding is included in Figure 10.3. Refer back to Box 3.2 for an explanation of the squares (pixels) that are visible in these highly magnified images.
- In addition to cryovolcanism, fracturing (faulting) has played a role in the resurfacing of Enceladus, Tethys and Dione. Fracturing of part of Dione is seen in Figure 10.4.

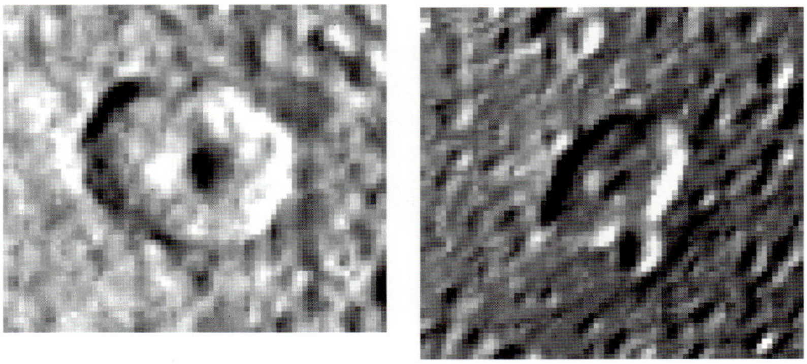

Figure 10.3 An enlargement of two parts of *TYP* Figure 10.10, showing (left) a 100 km diameter crater whose original raised rim is still prominent and (right) a 60 km diameter crater that appears to have been buried right up to the rim by cryovolcanic flooding of the surrounding plain. Look at this image from a distance if all you can see at first is a mass of squares (pixels).

Figure 10.4 Part of Dione, with a prominently visible fracture running southwards across the globe. The large (100 km diameter) crater with a central peak is the same one that can be seen near the upper edge of the globe in *TYP* Figure 10.11. The surface extending at least 50 km either side of the fracture has a lower density of impact craters than the region south and east of the large crater, and must have been resurfaced, presumably by cryovolcanic eruptions.

- Rhea is extremely heavily cratered, at least in the well-imaged portion of the globe (*TYP* Figure 10.12 and images on the S196 CD-ROM) and conforms most closely to what icy satellites were expected to look like before it was realized that tidal heating could lead to resurfacing.
- Titan is the only satellite of Saturn with a substantial atmosphere. This has hitherto prevented any clear view of its surface, which may include seas of liquid ethane. If all goes well, the truth will begin to be revealed when Cassini's Huygens probe lands in November 2004.
- Iapetus is particularly weird, and may turn out to have more in common with Centaur class asteroids (*TYP* p. 98) than with Saturn's regular satellites.

10.2 Chapter 10 questions

Now try to answer the following questions, to remind you of some of the things you have learned and test your understanding of them.

Question 10.1

Which two of the following features does Saturn not share with Jupiter?

A Hadley cells in its atmosphere

B A strong magnetic field whose axis is tilted relative to the planet's rotational axis

C Traces of phosphine (PH_3) in the atmosphere

D Rotating storm systems

E Rings made mostly of dusty particles micrometres in size

F Satellites in orbital resonance ◀

Question 10.2

Using the orbital periods in *TYP* Table 10.2, determine whether Mimas is in orbital resonance with either of the two other large satellites nearest to it, and comment on whether or not significant tidal heating occurs within Mimas. ◀

Question 10.3

According to *TYP*, why is there no oxygen gas in Titan's atmosphere?

A There are no oxygen-containing compounds on Titan's surface.

B All the oxygen has been used up to oxidize the rocks.

C Water-ice at the surface neither evaporates nor becomes split into hydrogen and oxygen by radiation.

D All the available oxygen is dissolved in liquid ethane. ◀

Question 10.4

List the following four satellites of Saturn in order of increasing signs of resurfacing (and by inference increasing tidal heating): Dione, Enceladus, Rhea, Tethys. ◀

Question 10.5

The IAU convention for names on Dione is to take them from Virgil's *Aeneid*, a Latin epic about exiles from Troy who eventually settled in Italy. The prominent fracture referred to in the caption for Figure 10.4 has been named Latium Chasma. Latium is taken from the name of the region in Italy where the Trojan exiles settled. What does the descriptor term 'chasma' imply, and do you think it is appropriate in this case? ◀

11 Uranus

Now study *TYP* Chapter 11, and return here when you have finished.

11.1 Discussion of Chapter 11

Please read the following discussion before attempting the questions in Section 11.2.

11.1.1 Uranus itself

Uranus's rock and ice core is hidden beneath nearly 10 000 km of mainly hydrogen. This is much less than in Jupiter and Saturn, hence the distinction made on *TYP* p. 16 between 'gas giants' (Jupiter and Saturn only) and 'giant planets' (encompassing all four of Jupiter, Saturn, Uranus and Neptune). Nevertheless, there is an awful lot of gas in Uranus, of which we can see only the outermost fringe.

Having reached Uranus, we are now come to the closest substantial planetary body that has been visited only once, by Voyager 2 during a flyby in 1986. At that time Uranus's south pole was pointed more or less directly towards the Sun (remember that its rotation axis is inclined at nearly 98° to its orbital plane).

- Look up Uranus's orbital period in the *Planetary facts* table on *TYP* p. 165, and estimate roughly when you would next expect the planet's poles to lie edge on to the Sun, so that the Sun is overhead at midday on the equator.

- Uranus's orbital period is about 84 years. If its south pole faced the Sun in 1986, its north pole will face the Sun half an orbit (42 years) later. The poles will be edge-on to the Sun half way between these times, i.e. 21 years after 1986, which is in the year 2007. (Uranus's orbit is sufficiently close to circular that we can ignore variable orbital speed with distance from the Sun, as expressed by Kepler's second law, in this simple estimate.)

You can see from the concentric pattern of Uranus's otherwise rather featureless atmosphere in *TYP* Figure 11.1 that the south pole was indeed pointed sunwards in 1986. Large-scale atmospheric circulation at this time, which is poorly expressed by any visible features, was presumably operating to redistribute heat from the sunlit pole towards the hemisphere in darkness. However, by the time of the 1998 Hubble Space Telescope image in Figure 11.1 here, a large part of the northern hemisphere had come into sunlight, though the north pole would not see the Sun for a further nine years. The atmosphere was no longer so bland as in 1986, with the development of isolated high-altitude clouds believed to be of methane ice crystals and analogous to cirrus clouds in Earth's atmosphere. Perhaps Uranus will develop a Jupiter-like (and Saturn-like) pattern of Hadley circulation during the few years when it lies side-on to the Sun.

The colours in Figure 11.1 are not real, but they still contain useful information. In this case, colours on the planet relate to the depth of atmosphere above the cloud tops, because the deeper we see, the more long-wavelength infrared is absorbed (mainly by methane gas). Thus in this rendering the bluer the colour, the deeper we see. The bright pinkish spots in northern latitudes are high clouds, above the main cloud layer. The rings show up more clearly than they would in an image recorded at visible wavelengths, because they reflect more strongly in the near-infrared. Uranus3 on the S196 CD-ROM uses a slightly different combination of wavelengths in another false-colour composite to reveal additional cloud-top height information.

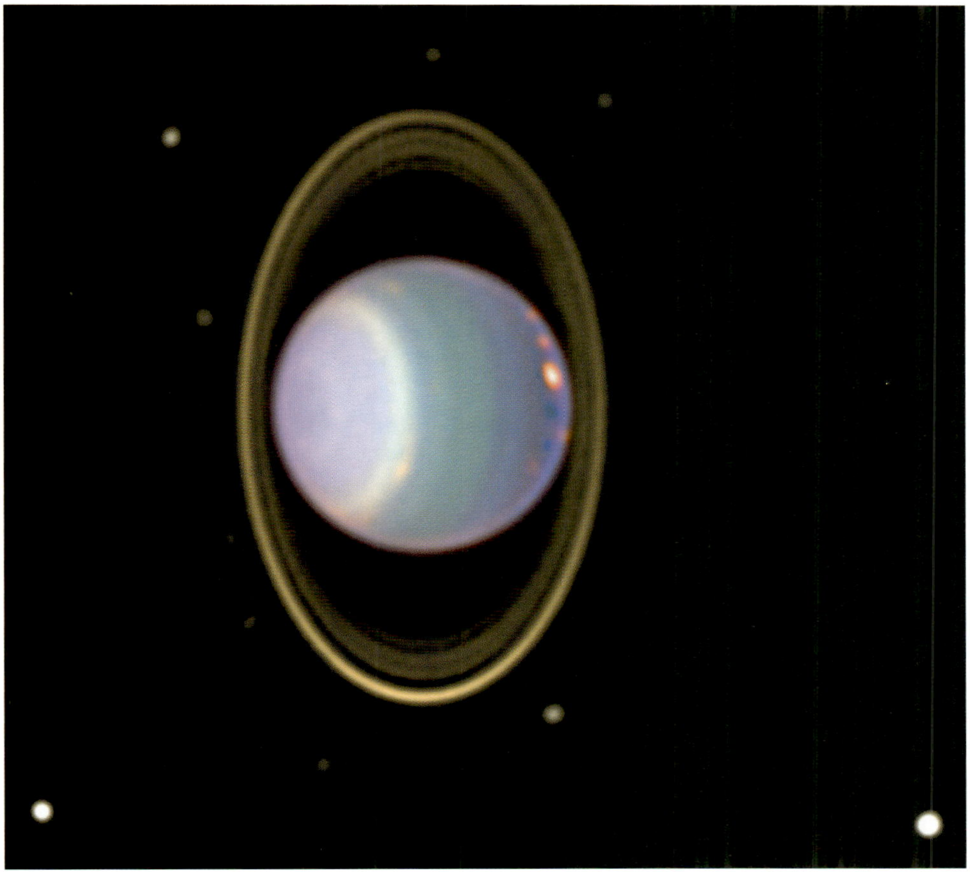

Figure 11.1 A false-colour infrared image of Uranus and ten of its satellites recorded by the Hubble Space Telescope in August 1998. Red, green and blue in this image represent near-infrared radiation at 1700, 1100 and 900 nm. The rings show up well at these long wavelengths, although they would be very faint in visible light.

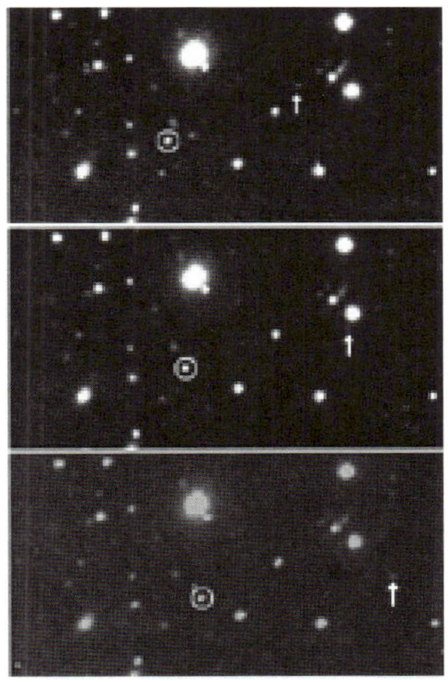

Figure 11.2 The discovery images of Sycorax, which were made on 6 September 1997 using the 200 inch (5 metre) Hale telescope at the famous Palomar Observatory in California. The superimposed circle locates Sycorax, and the position of a fainter and faster moving asteroid is indicated by the arrow. Uranus itself is out of the field of view.

- How far beyond the visible part of the spectrum is the shortest wavelength that has been used to construct Figure 11.1?

- According to Box 3.3, visible light is from 400 nm (blue) to 700 nm (red) in wavelength. The shortest wavelength used in Figure 11.1 is 900 nm, which is 200 nm beyond the visible spectrum.

11.1.2 Rings and the satellite family

Uranus's rings have much more mass than Jupiter's, though less than Saturn's. One estimate for their total mass is about 10^{16} kg. You may note in Figure 11.1 here that the brightness of the outer ring (the epsilon ring) varies around its circumference. This is related to the variable width of the ring mentioned on *TYP* p.169, but which cannot be seen directly on this image because the ring is too narrow to be resolved and appears on this image to be far wider than it actually is. *TYP* Figure 11.3 reveals the true narrowness of this ring and also shows the two shepherd satellites that confine it. It is likely that undiscovered shepherd satellites only a few kilometres across are responsible for maintaining the narrowness of each of the other rings too.

Uranus's satellite family conforms nicely to the giant planet pattern discussed on *TYP* p. 121. Many of the inner moonlets can be seen in Figure 11.1, and the discovery images of the largest irregular outer satellite are shown in Figure 11.2.

11.1.3 Individual satellites

The Voyager project did not produce such good images of Uranus's regular satellites as it did at Saturn. This is partly because only one of the two Voyagers visited Uranus after Saturn, but mostly because of the tilt of Uranus's axis.

- At the time of the fly-by, Uranus's south pole was pointing roughly towards the direction from which Voyager 2 arrived. What does this tell you about the orientation of the orbits of the regular satellites relative to Voyager's trajectory?

- Regular satellites have orbits lying almost exactly in the plane of their planet's equator. Thus these orbits made a bull's-eye pattern of concentric circles roughly perpendicular to Voyager's trajectory.

You can see this bull's-eye pattern as it appeared from Earth in 1994 if you look at the movie Uranus10 on the S196 CD-ROM, which is constructed from Hubble Space Telescope images. The five satellites visible at the beginning are the five regular satellites, but as the movie plays the view zooms in to reveal many of the inner moonlets. A zoomed-in movie taken four years later, with a discernible difference in orientation of the rings and satellite orbits relative to Earth, is shown in Uranus11.

Had Voyager encountered the orbits edge-on, as at Jupiter and Saturn's regular satellites, it would have been possible to arrange its passage through the system so as to cross each orbit and to do so at a time when each satellite was relatively nearby. However, the bull's-eye pattern meant that Voyager could pass close to only one of the satellites. Miranda was chosen, because this was the innermost previously discovered satellite, and this would also take Voyager close to Uranus itself. Consequently, Voyager did not pass particularly near any of the other regular satellites. The highest resolution images of Miranda have pixels only about 600 m across, but this increases to 2.4 km at Ariel, a little less than 10 km at Umbriel and Titania, and 12 km at Oberon.

There are currently no orbital resonances among Uranus's regular satellites, but two of them (Miranda and Ariel) show clear signs of ancient cryovolcanic resurfacing (Figures 11.3 and 11.4), suggesting that tidal heating may have operated during episodes of orbital resonance in the distant past (at least a billion years ago). However, it is not essential to invoke tidal heating to explain the fracturing or even the cryovolcanic resurfacing. *TYP* pp. 176–179 hint at two other possible causes: freezing of a previously molten part of the interior could lead to slight expansion in the volume of the globe and hence stretching and fracturing of the surface, or else fractures could be generated by tidal forces (irrespective of any tidal heating). Once fractures had been generated, these could act as pathways for the escape of any molten material that happened still to remain in the interior. Ariel could be an example of a fractured surface onto which cryovolcanic magmas escaped, whereas Titania could be an example of a fractured surface with little or no subsequent cryovolcanic flooding.

- Bearing in mind the direction from which the Sun is shining in Figure 11.4, what is the nature of the topographic feature that runs from X to Y?

- This is a broad valley, with a flattish bottom and steep walls. The right-hand wall, which faces left, is illuminated by the Sun and so appears bright. The left-hand wall, which faces right, and therefore away from the Sun, is partly in shadow.

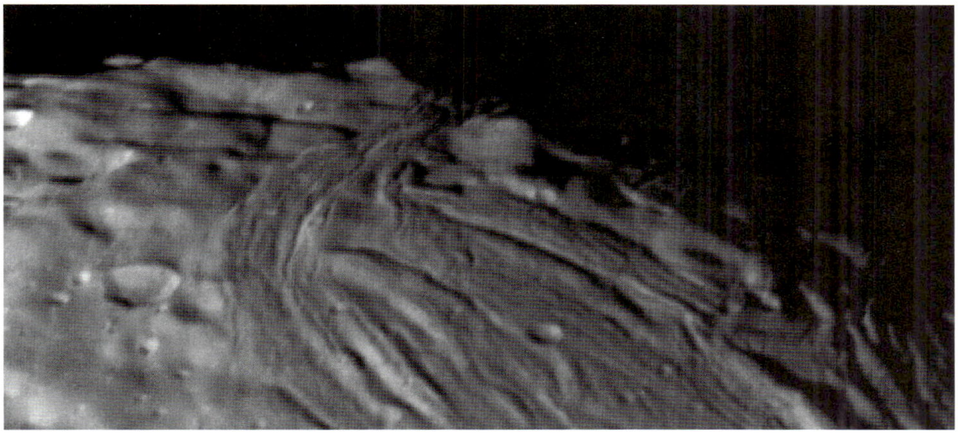

Figure 11.3 A 100 km wide region of Miranda, extracted from the upper right of *TYP* Figure 11.6. Solar illumination is from the lower left. Most of this region appears to have been resurfaced by cryovolcanic lava flows.

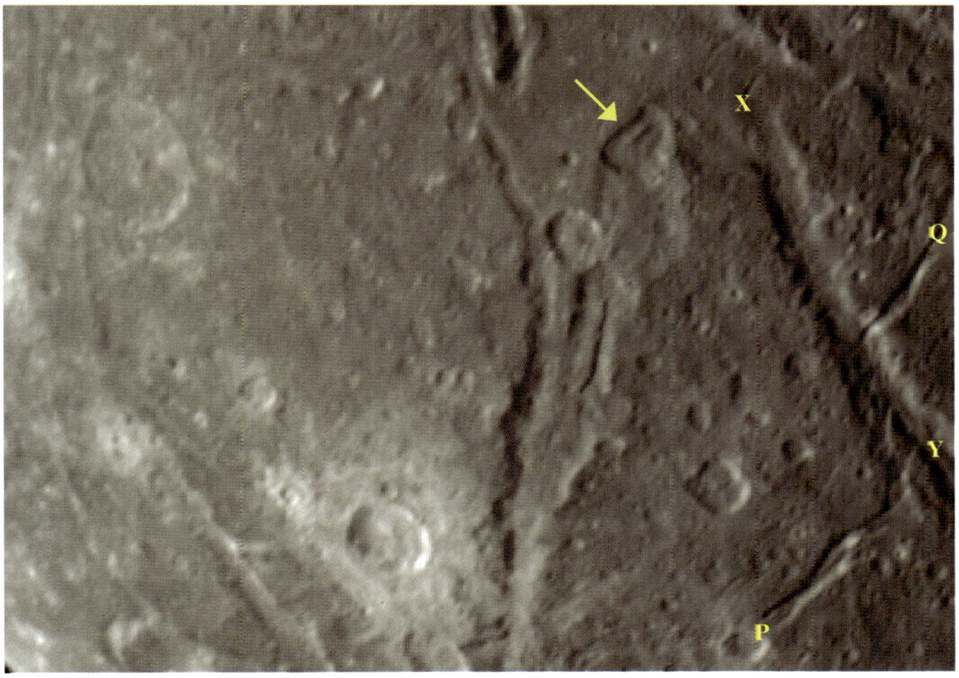

Figure 11.4 A 600 km wide region of Ariel, extracted from the lower part of *TYP* Figure 11.8. Solar illumination is from the left. The arrow indicates an ancient impact crater whose upper left portion appears to have been buried by a viscous cryovolcanic flow. The letters are referred to in the text.

If you interpreted the feature X–Y as a ridge rather than as a valley, you were probably imagining the illumination shining from the right rather than from the left. The relative straightness of the valley walls is probably because they are faults, representing fractures that allowed the valley floor to drop downwards. The feature between P and Q is addressed in Question 11.4.

The cryovolcanic lava flows on Miranda and Ariel are thick and steep-sided, which indicates that they were gooey in consistency rather than free-flowing. In other words their viscosity was high. This is a strong indicator of the presence of ammonia within the melted material. Ammonia has not been detected spectroscopically (this would be very hard to do), but it is among the contaminants that we expect to be mixed with water-ice in this distant part of the Solar System (*TYP* p. 19). The resolution of the images of Titania is too poor to show cryovolcanic features, but major fractures can be seen that may attest to similar events.

11.2 Chapter 11 questions

Now try to answer the following questions, to remind you of some of the things you have learned and test your understanding of them.

Question 11.1

Which one of the following features does Uranus share with Jupiter?

A Metallic hydrogen in its interior

B A strong magnetic field whose axis is tilted relative to the planet's rotational axis

C Traces of phosphine (PH_3) in the atmosphere

D Rotating storm systems

E Rings made mostly of dusty particles micrometres in size

F Satellites in orbital resonance

G A topmost cloud layer of ammonia ice crystals ◀

Question 11.2

As for Saturn's rings, the predominance of boulders among Uranus's ring material has been deduced from their effect on radio signals travelling between Voyager and Earth. However, how is the presence of dust demonstrated? ◀

Question 11.3

The IAU naming convention for features on Ariel is to use the names of light (as opposed to dark) spirits from folklore of various cultures. Feature X–Y on Figure 11.4 is named Korrigan, after wind spirits in Breton folklore. What descriptor term from Table 2.1 do you think would be appropriate to complete the name? ◀

Question 11.4

The feature running from P to Q on Figure 11.4 is named Kra Chasma (Kra being spirits in the folklore of the Gold Coast of West Africa). Look carefully at the relationship between Kra Chasma and Korrigan Chasma (X–Y). Can you tell which is the older of the two? ◀

Neptune

12

Now study *TYP* Chapter 12, and return here when you have finished.

12.1 Discussion of Chapter 12

Please read the following discussion before attempting the questions in Section 12.2.

12.1.1 Neptune itself

Neptune's internal structure is believed to resemble Uranus's, but there are several differences. Answer Question 12.1 to check if you have digested or can find the relevant information.

Question 12.1

Which of the following statements is/are wrong?

A Neptune generates more heat than Uranus.

B Neptune is not tilted on its side like Uranus.

C Neptune's visible clouds are ammonia, unlike Uranus's.

D The centre of symmetry of Neptune's magnetic field is closer to the surface than Uranus's.

E At the time of the Voyager encounters, Neptune's atmosphere showed more visual structure than Uranus's.

F Neptune radiates more heat than it receives from the Sun, unlike Uranus. ◀

Neptune was certainly a glorious sight when Voyager 2 flew past, especially when seen in colour as in *TYP* Plate 11 and Figure 12.1 here, in contrast to the relatively featureless state of Uranus recorded by the same probe three and a half years previously. However, as discussed in Section 11.1.1, Uranus's appearance has undergone seasonal change associated with its extreme axial tilt. If you compare recent Hubble Space Telescope images such as Uranus2 and 3 with Neptune5 and 13 on the S196 CD-ROM, you will see that the planets look much more alike than they do on Voyager images.

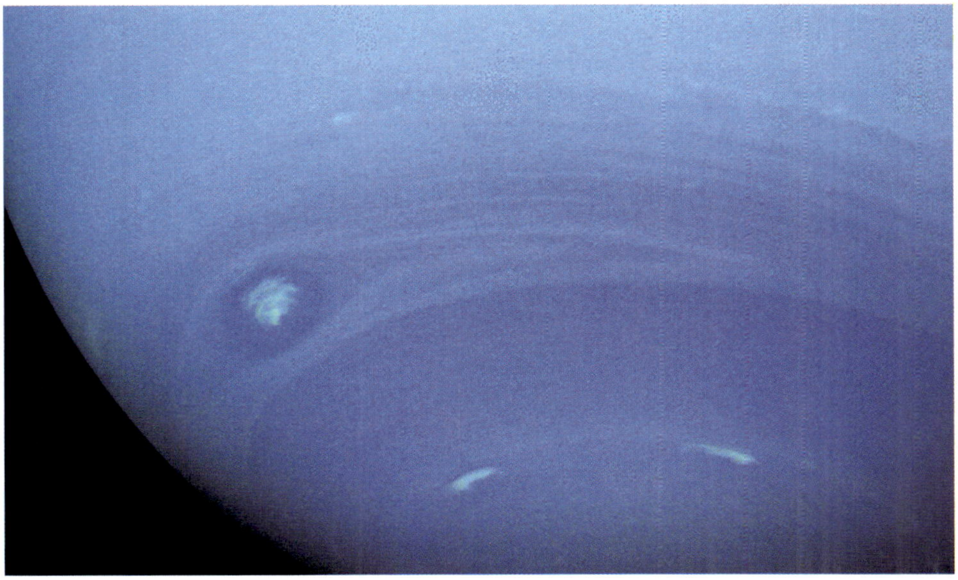

Figure 12.1 Part of Neptune's southern hemisphere, seen in almost natural colour by Voyager 2. The Small Dark Spot is obvious. Except for this rotating storm system, the winds in the cloud layer, indicated by faint streaking of the atmosphere, follow lines of latitude. South of the Small Dark Spot winds blow westwards at up to 200 metres per second, whereas north of it they blow eastwards, peaking at over 300 metres per second near the equator. This is presumably Hadley circulation, deflected by the planet's rotation.

It is unlikely that Neptune's Great Dark Spot and Small Dark Spot would have been named without the historical precedent set by Jupiter's Great Red Spot. Neptune's spots seem to be much shorter-lived than Jupiter's famous example. So far as can be told from Hubble Space Telescope images, the Great Dark Spot had gone by 1994, whereas a new dark spot of similar size had appeared in the northern hemisphere at a similar latitude. This can be seen on Neptune4 and 5 on the S196 CD-ROM, where it is picked out by the associated high-altitude clouds.

12.1.2 Rings and the satellite family

Neptune has the least substantial ring system of all the giant planets (Figure 12.2). Several of the inner satellites are within the ring system and may act as shepherds that keep the ring material confined (see Table 12.1). Shepherd satellites may also be responsible for the bunching of the material of the Adams ring into arcs (*TYP* Figure 12.5).

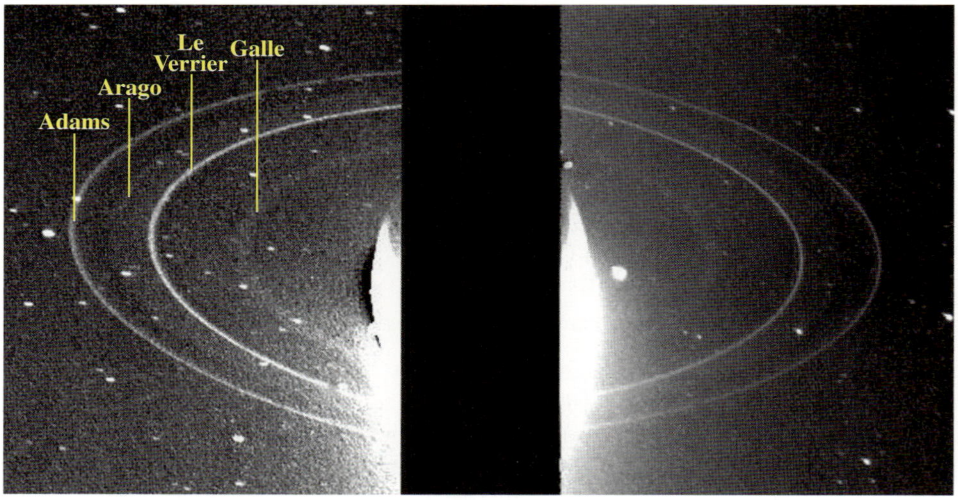

Figure 12.2 A montage of two images of Neptune's rings seen in forward-scattered light by Voyager 2 from a range of 280 000 km, as it receded from Neptune. Each exposure was nearly ten minutes and so the image of Neptune is greatly overexposed, even though it would have appeared as a slender crescent. This enables the extremely faint rings to show up. Four of them have been labelled with their names. The fifth ring, the Lassell ring, is a tenuous ring extending outwards from the LeVerrier ring to just beyond the Arago ring.

Table 12.1 Radii, widths and thicknesses of Neptune's rings.

Name	Distance from Neptune's centre (km)	Radial width (km)	Thickness (km)
Galle	41 900	15	?
LeVerrier	53 200	110	<30
Lassell	53 200–59 100	4000	?
Arago	57 200	<100	?
Adams	62 930	<50	<30

- Compare the ring radii (distances from Neptune's centre) in Table 12.1 with the satellite orbits in *TYP* Table 12.1 (p. 191). Which of these satellites have orbits lying less than 1000 km from a ring, and are therefore likely to act as shepherd satellites?

- Despina, whose orbit is only about 670 km within the LeVerrier ring, and Galatea, whose orbit is only about 980 km within the Adams ring.

There may be numerous undiscovered shepherd satellites, probably including at least one orbiting just outside the LeVerrier ring and another just outside the Adams ring. As noted on *TYP* p. 190, it is now clear that Galatea alone cannot be responsible for the Adams ring arcs. Figure 12.3 here shows one of the post-Voyager telescope images that were used to demonstrate this.

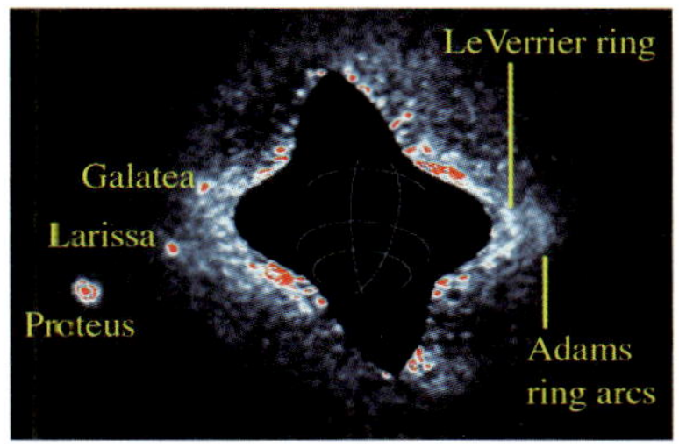

Figure 12.3 An image of the Neptune system recorded over 90 minutes on 6 July 1998 by a telescope in Hawaii using a procedure called 'adaptive optics' to correct for the shimmering effect of the Earth's atmosphere. Neptune has been masked out (though some glare still remains) and its position is indicated by the faint outline of latitude and longitude. Ring arc 'clumps' in the Adams ring have drifted out of the position they should have been in if they were controlled simply by orbital resonance with Galatea.

Neptune's five innermost known satellites appear to be conventional inner moonlets. Nereid has an inclined (though not retrograde) and extremely eccentric distant orbit, and would appear to be a large but otherwise fairly unremarkable irregular outer satellite. However, both Proteus and Triton mark Neptune's satellite family as unusual. Proteus would be a normal regular satellite except that despite (slightly) exceeding 200 km in radius its shape is distinctly non-spherical. Maybe this is a result of a near catastrophic collision, in which case Proteus could be the badly scared sole-survivor of a group of regular satellites whose other members were flung out or destroyed by collisions when the interloper Triton arrived. However, as *TYP* p. 192 suggests, Nereid could be the remains of a survivor too.

The discovery of the three small irregular outer satellites S/2002 N1, N2 and N3 was announced in January 2003. Because of this I had to make some very late revisions to *TYP*. To give you a flavour of the information available at such early stages, Box 12.1 reproduces part of the press release issued on behalf of part of the team that made the discovery.

Box 12.1 New moons found around Neptune

Harvard-Smithsonian Center for Astrophysics

Press Release No.: 03-03

For Release: January 13, 2003

Cambridge, MA - A team of astronomers led by Matthew Holman (Harvard-Smithsonian Center for Astrophysics) and JJ Kavelaars (National Research Council of Canada) has discovered three previously unknown moons of Neptune. This boosts the number of known satellites of the gas giant to eleven. These moons are the first to be discovered orbiting Neptune since the Voyager II flyby in 1989, and the first discovered from a ground-based telescope since 1949.

It now appears that each giant planet's irregular satellite population is the result of an ancient collision between a former moon and a passing comet or asteroid. 'These collisional encounters result in the ejection of parts of the original parent moon and the production of families of satellites. Those families are exactly what we're finding,' said Kavelaars.

The team that discovered these new satellites of Neptune includes Holman and Kavelaars, graduate student Tommy Grav (University of Oslo & Harvard-Smithsonian Center for Astrophysics), and undergraduate students Wesley Fraser and Dan Milisavljevic (McMaster University, Hamilton, Ontario, Canada).

The word 'magnitude' in this press release is an astronomical term to denote the brightness of objects seen in the sky. The *higher* the magnitude the fainter the object appears.

Needle in a Haystack

The new satellites were a challenge to detect because they are only about 30-40 kilometers (18-24 miles) in size. Their small size and distance from the Sun prevent the satellites from shining any brighter than 25th magnitude, about 100 million times fainter than can be seen with the unaided eye.

To locate these new moons, Holman and Kavelaars utilized an innovative technique. Using the 4.0-meter Blanco telescope at the Cerro Tololo Inter-American Observatory, Chile, and the 3.6-meter Canada-France-Hawaii Telescope, Hawaii, they took multiple exposures of the sky surrounding the planet Neptune. After digitally tracking the motion of the planet as it moved across the sky, they then added many frames together to boost the signal of any faint objects. Since they tracked the planet's motion, stars showed up in the final combined image as streaks of light, while the moons accompanying the planet appeared as points of light.

Prior to this find, two irregular satellites and six regular satellites of Neptune were known. The two irregular satellites were also the largest: Triton, discovered in 1846 by William Lassell, and Nereid, discovered in 1949 by Gerard Kuiper. Triton is considered irregular because it orbits the planet in a direction opposite to the planet's rotation, indicating that Triton is likely a captured Kuiper Belt Object. (The Kuiper Belt is a disk-shaped collection of icy objects that circle the Sun beyond the orbit of Neptune.) Nereid is considered irregular because it has a highly elliptical orbit around Neptune. In fact, its orbit is the most elliptical of any satellite in the solar system. Many scientists believe that Nereid once was a regular satellite whose orbit was disrupted when Triton was gravitationally captured. The six regular satellites were discovered by the Voyager probe during its encounter with Neptune. The three new satellites were missed by Voyager 2 because of their faintness and great distance from Neptune. According to Holman, 'The discovery of these moons has opened a window through which we can observe the conditions in the solar system at the time the planets were forming.'

The researchers are currently conducting follow-up observations to better define the orbits of the newfound moons. Holman says, 'Tracking these moons is an enormous, international undertaking involving the efforts of many people. Without teamwork, such faint objects could be easily lost.'

12.1.3 Triton

Triton is a fascinating place, with a complicated geological history. The images in *TYP* Figures 12.7–12.9, Plate 12 and the S196 CD-ROM hint at the variety of processes that have shaped it surface. Triton's orbital eccentricity has been determined to five significant figures as 0.0000, making it indistinguishable from a circle, so there is no known mechanism to cause tidal heating today on Triton. However, the geological complexity of its surface makes it seem highly likely that tidal heating must have operated in the past.

- *TYP* p. 191 states that Triton is 'clearly a captured body'. What is the simplest and strongest evidence for this?

Triton's orbit is retrograde. This is incompatible with growth from a disc of dust and gas around the young planet in the manner described for the regular satellites on *TYP* p. 17, because such a disc would have to have been rotating in the same direction as the planet.

Other evidence that supports (but cannot, in isolation, prove) this is:

- Triton's tidal heating (deduced from its resurfacing history) which would follow from capture, at a time when tides were forcing its orbit into a circular shape and slowing its rotation until it became synchronous with its orbital period.
- Triton's compositional similarity to objects still in the Kuiper belt, such as Pluto.

Triton has a seasonally variable atmosphere in common with Pluto. *TYP* does not illustrate the atmosphere, but it can be seen here in Figure 12.4.

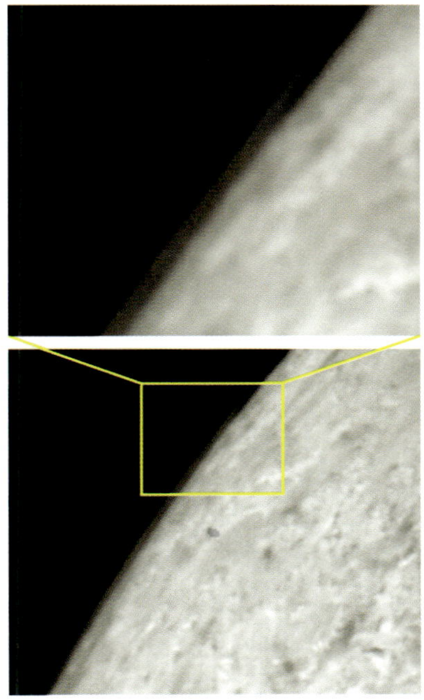

Figure 12.4 A Voyager 2 image of the edge of Triton's disc above its south polar cap, with the contrast exaggerated to reveal a layer of clouds of nitrogen ice at about 13 km altitude, analogous to cirrus clouds in the Earth's atmosphere.

12.2 Chapter 12 questions

Now try to answer the following questions, to remind you of some of the things you have learned and test your understanding of them.

Question 12.2

The first paragraph of the press release in Box 12.1 refers to Neptune as a 'gas giant'. Do you think that is correct? ◀

Question 12.3

Which features in the following list are believed to occur on Triton but not on Enceladus?

A Resurfacing of a variety of ages

B Solar-powered geysers

C Cantaloupe terrain

D Impact craters

E Nitrogen ice

F Present-day tidal heating ◀

Question 12.4

Features on Triton are given aquatic names from global cultures, excluding Latin and Greek. Figure 12.5 shows part of Triton from within the area shown in *TYP* Figure 12.8, which you can probably also locate within the top right of Plate 12. The feature running between X and Y is named Slidr (after a river from Norse mythology) and the feature P–Q is named Tano (a name from the Yaruba culture of west Africa). Both names are completed by the same descriptor term. Which descriptor term from Table 2.1 do you think would be appropriate? ◀

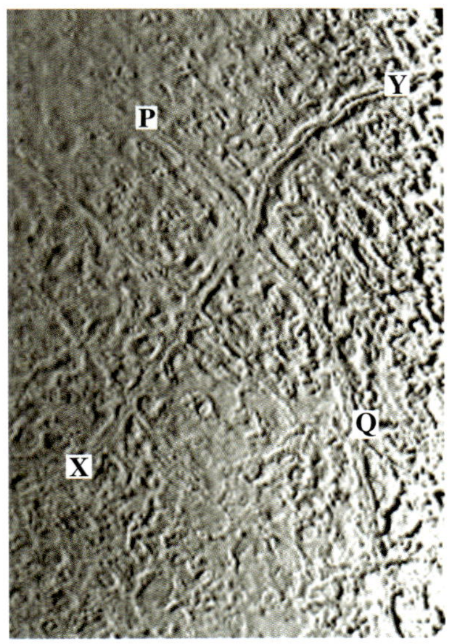

Figure 12.5 Part of Triton about 400 km across. Solar illumination is from the left. For use with Question 12.4.

Question 12.5

Suggest a reason why Triton's south polar cap of nitrogen ice sublimes rather than melts in the spring. ◀

13 Pluto, Charon and the Kuiper belt

Now study *TYP* Chapter 13, and return here when you have finished.

13.1 Discussion of Chapter 13

Please read the following comments before attempting the questions in Section 13.2.

13.1.1 Pluto and Charon

- Pluto's discovery (Figure 13.1) was a result of a dedicated search for a much more massive body, which is now known not to exist. Before finding Pluto, the Lowell Observatory search programme also discovered one comet and 775 asteroids.
- Pluto–Charon is probably just a large double Kuiper belt object. However, it is possible that Pluto has an unusual origin, such as being a former regular satellite of Neptune that escaped when Triton was captured.
- Spectroscopic data show that Pluto's atmosphere and surface are fairly Triton-like in composition. Although they are remarkable achievements, the telescopic images that show surface albedo patterns have far too low resolution to give us much inkling of the physical nature of the surface. Look at the comparable resolution image of the Moon in *TYP* Figure 13.1 and consider how little this alone would tell us when compared with the images of the Moon in Chapter 6.
- No ice other than water has been detected on Charon. *TYP* p. 205 suggests two possible reasons why these more volatile species are lacking. An alternative explanation could be that Charon actually does have these species in considerable abundance but that they have not been detected because Charon is exceptionally hard to observe separately, being so close to Pluto.

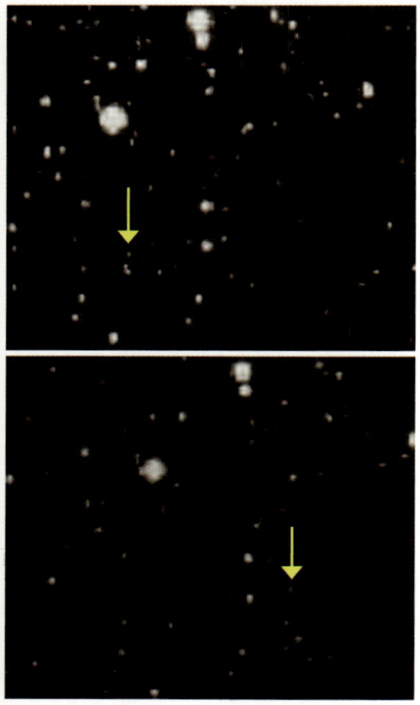

Figure 13.1 The discovery photographs of Pluto taken on 23 (above) and 29 (below) January 1930. Pluto is indicated by an arrow, and can be seen to have moved relative to the background stars (mainly as a result of changing perspective due to the Earth's orbital motion). Other differences between the two views are mainly because the 29 January photograph does not show quite such faint stars.

13.1.2 The Kuiper belt

All Trans-Neptunian objects belonging to the Solar System are challenging to observe, on account of their distance, generally low albedo and relatively small size. The discovery images of 1992 QB_1 are reproduced in Figure 13.2, and you will find various others on the S196 CD-ROM.

This section of *TYP* was heavily revised between editions. Even so, *TYP* Tables 13.1 and 13.2, which list the largest known Trans-Neptunian objects and those known to have satellites, will inevitably be out of date by the time you read this. You can find more up-to-date information from Internet sites such as http://www.boulder.swri.edu/ekonews/ and http://www.hohmanntransfer.com/news.htm.

TYP p. 208 mentions that it seems unlikely that the probable number of double objects can be explained as a result of giant impacts. The reason for this is that statistically such collisions should be too rare. However, two objects that simply stray close to each other without colliding cannot become orbitally bound into a double object, because to do so would require a loss of momentum that cannot be achieved if just two objects are involved. The solution to the conundrum may be to involve a third object, such that all three pass close together at the same time, as illustrated in the animation KBO7 on the S196 CD-ROM. The bodies must pass so close that their mutual gravitational attraction exceeds the gravitational pull from the Sun, which for a 100 km diameter object in the Kuiper belt requires an approach within about a million kilometres. When this happens, about one time in a hundred, two of the bodies can lose sufficient momentum to the third that they become bound whereas the third departs the scene at a slighter higher speed than it arrived. Alternatively, the role of the third body could be taken by a number of smaller bodies.

The process of capture and subsequent interaction between the newly bound pair could lead to enough tidal heating for them to become internally differentiated and maybe power an episode of cryovolcanism on their surfaces. This is a fascinating prospect, but we must await the success of the New Horizons mission and its successors before we know for sure.

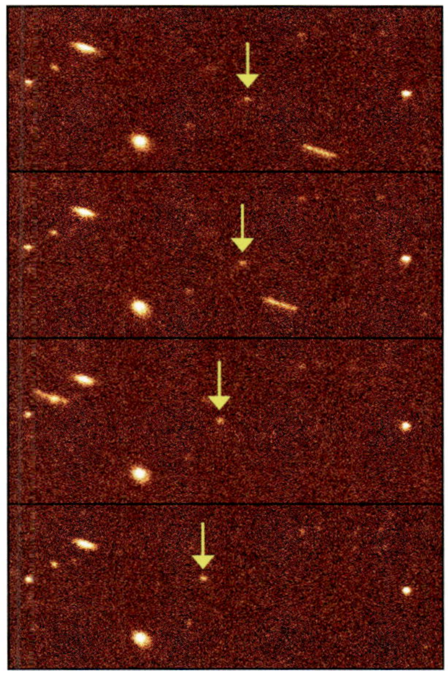

Figure 13.2 The discovery images of 1992 QB_1, in a series of four taken over a period of 205 minutes. 1992 QB_1 is indicated by the arrow. It is overtaken by a much faster moving asteroid that appears as a blurred streak in the first three images.

13.1.3 Beyond the Kuiper belt

The final section of the chapter mentions the theory that there is a Jupiter-mass object about 32 000 AU from the Sun that is responsible for dislodging long-period comets so that they swoop sunwards from their normal home in the Oort cloud. By April 2003 the search programme for this body had got as far a collecting suitable images of 40% of the appropriate area of sky. This had revealed a few dozen candidate objects requiring confirmation by re-imaging, most of which are likely to turn out be false alarms. For the time being, the existence of such a body remains conjectural.

13.2 Chapter 13 questions

Now try to answer the following questions, to remind you of some of the things you have learned and test your understanding of them.

Question 13.1

Which of the following statements is/are correct?

A Pluto–Charon is the only double object in the Kuiper belt.

B Charon is known to have a seasonally variable atmosphere.

C Charon's orbit about the Pluto–Charon barycentre (centre of mass) appears to be exactly circular.

D Pluto is more massive than Triton.

E Charon could be undergoing tidal heating today. ◀

Question 13.2

With the aid of Table 8.1, deduce, as fully as possible, the date when 1992 QB_1 was discovered. ◀

Question 13.3

2002 TC_{302} is a fairly large Trans-Neptunian object that failed to make it into *TYP* Table 13.1, but which may exceed 400 km in radius. On the basis of the following figures describing its orbit, decide to which class of Trans-Neptunian objects it belongs: mean distance from Sun, 55.7 AU; orbital period, 415 years; orbital eccentricity, 0.300; orbital inclination, 35.1°. ◀

14 Planets round other stars

Now study *TYP* Chapter 14, and return here when you have finished.

14.1 Discussion of Chapter 14

Please read the following comments before attempting the questions in Sections 14.2 and 14.3.

14.1.1 Detecting exoplanets

TYP p. 212 mentions observations of dust discs surrounding young stars that could be analogues of the solar nebula from which grew the Earth and the Sun's other planets. One example is shown here in Figure 14.1, and you will find others on the S196 CD-ROM under the heading *Planet Formation*.

In this course we do not expect you to understand more than the bare principles of how planets around other stars can be detected. The main thing to remember is that the most successful technique so far, the radial velocity method, favours detection of *massive* planets orbiting *close* to their stars, so you should not be surprised by the large masses and close orbits mentioned in the text. Figure 14.2 shows an example of radial velocity data for the star 51 Pegasi, which should give you a general impression of how the technique works, and Box 14.1 tells you all you need to know about how exoplanets are 'named'.

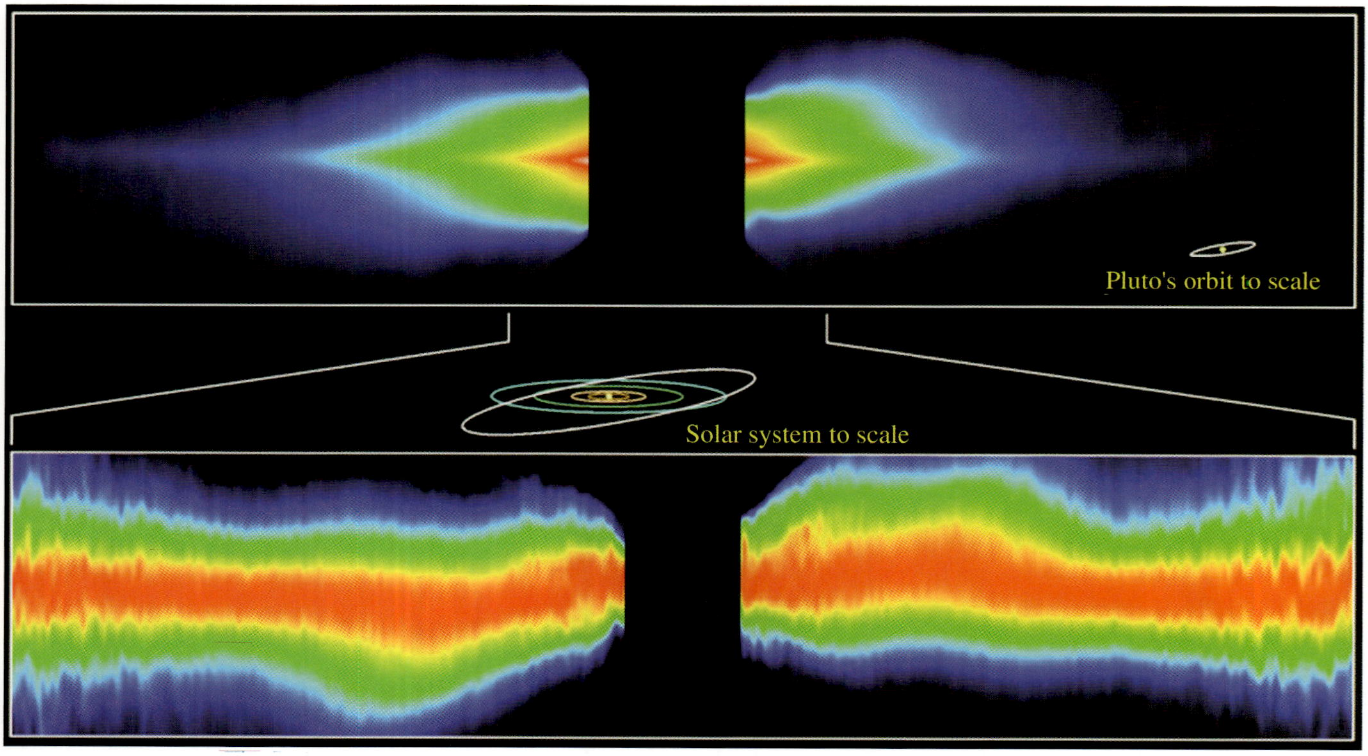

Figure 14.1 Two images from the Hubble Space Telescope showing the dust disc surrounding the young star Beta Pictoris. The disc appears edge-on as seen from Earth, and is made visible by the faint reflection of light from Beta Pictoris itself. In both images the disc has been colour-coded according to brightness but the glare from the star has been deliberately removed by the black strip across the middle. Top: the full extent of the disk. Bottom: the inner region of the disc.

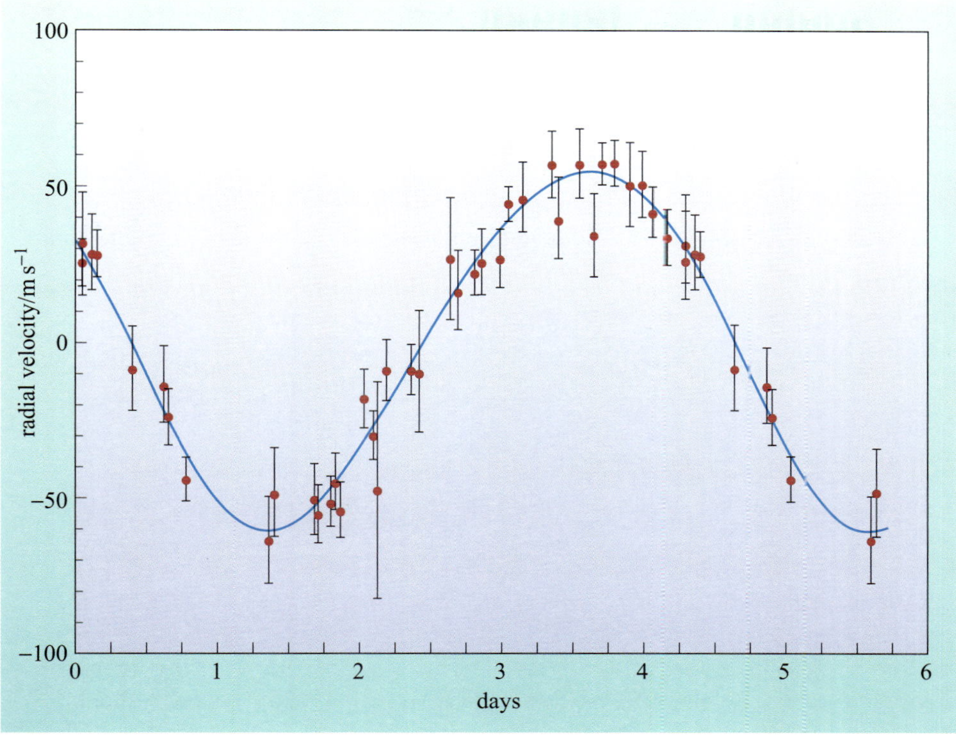

Figure 14.2 A graph of how the radial velocity of 51 Pegasi (corrected for the Earth's motion) varies with time. The points are individual measurements and the bars extending above and below each point represent the amount of uncertainty in that measurement. The blue line shows that the actual pattern of radial velocity change that can be deduced from this.

Box 14.1 Names of exoplanets

Exoplanets are not given independent names of their own, but have a designation based on the star that they orbit.

Stars that appear bright from the Earth are given a Greek letter or a number plus the name of the constellation in which they occur. Beta Pictoris and 51 Pegasi are examples of star names of this kind. Fainter stars are usually known by the name of the catalogue in which they are listed plus their catalogue number. Gliese 876 is an example of this kind.

When a planet is discovered around a star, it receives a designation consisting of its star's name plus a lower case letter of the alphabet. The letter 'a' is not used, so the first planet to be discovered receives the letter 'b', the second 'c', and so on. If several planets are discovered simultaneously letters are awarded in sequence working outwards from the star.

Thus the only known planet of 51 Pegasi is known as 51 Pegasi b.

The orbital period for 51 Pegasi's single detected planet as revealed by the regularly repeating pattern of radial velocity in Figure 14.2 is 4.23 days. From knowledge of the star's mass we can deduce that the planet orbits at a distance of 0.05 AU, and from the amount by which the star's position wobbles (as revealed by radial velocity changes) we can deduce that the planet's mass is 0.44 Jupiter-masses if its orbital plane is exactly edge-on to our line of sight. Its mass must be somewhat greater if the orbit is inclined. The symmetrical shape of the radial velocity curve in Figure 14.2 allows us to deduce that the planet's orbit must be virtually circular.

For any exoplanet, orbital period and average distance from the star are, of course, related. However, unless the star's mass is exactly the same as the mass of the Sun, the value of k in Kepler's third law (Equation 2.1) is not the same as for a planet in our own solar system.

The radial velocity method allows us to detect and measure the motion of a star towards and away from us as a planet goes round it. As *TYP* p. 212 remarks, any related changes in the star's position in the sky (representing motion at right angles to our line of sight) are much more challenging to detect because the wobble in the star's position is so slight. This so-called astrometric measurement was first achieved in 2002 for the star Gliese 876, which the radial velocity method had previously identified as having two planets, the more massive being at least 1.9 Jupiter-masses orbiting at 0.21 AU. Figure 14.3 illustrates the principles of the astrometric technique.

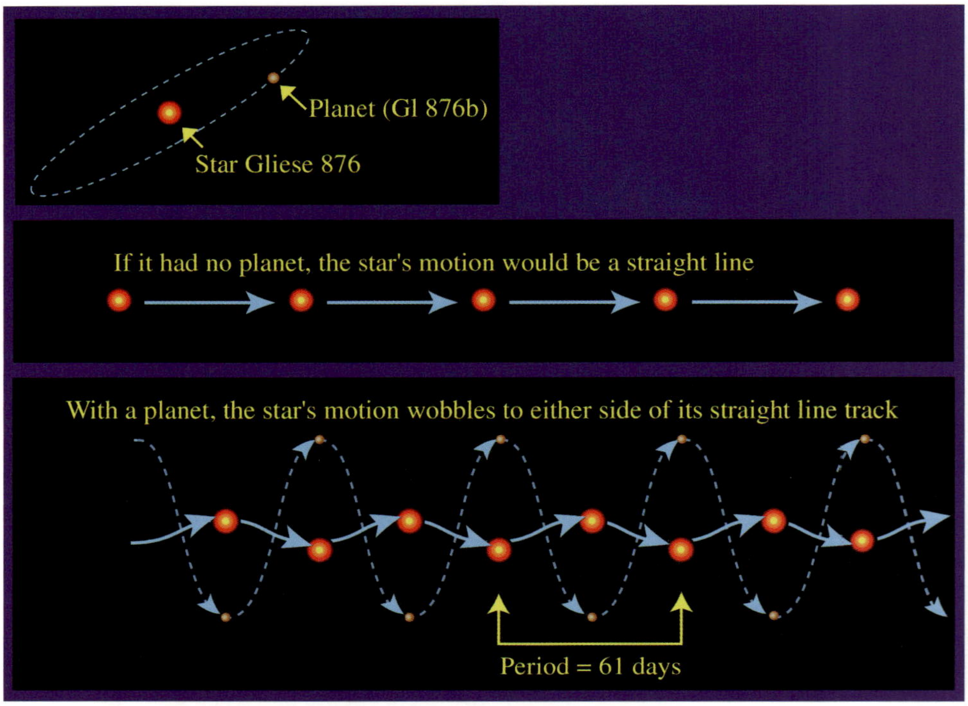

Figure 14.3 Astrometric detection of the wobble in the motion of Gliese 876 by very precise measurements of the star's position using the Hubble Space Telescope. In this case the wobble is only about 1.4×10^{-7} of a degree. The planet is invisible, but its presence can be deduced from the star's wobble.

In the case of Gliese 876 the astrometric technique worked because the star is relatively close to the Sun (about 15 light years or 1.4×10^{14} km away) and has a low mass, only about a third that of the Sun.

- Can you suggest why these two factors should make it easier to detect changes in a star's position?

- The closer the star is to us, the larger the displacement will appear to be in the sky. The lower the mass of the star, the greater the actual size of its displacement relative to the gravitational attraction of its planet.

Note that, in contrast to the astrometric method, the efficacy of the radial velocity method is independent of how far away the star is.

Astrometric detection of the wobble in the motion of Gliese 876 pushed the Hubble Space Telescope close to its limit. However, we can expect a flood of new data from some forthcoming satellites designed to measure stellar positions with a precision of about 1×10^{-8} of a degree. The first will be a NASA satellite called FAME (Full-sky Astrometric Mapping Explorer) planned for launch in 2004, and the next may be a European Space Agency satellite called Gaia in 2012.

As described in *TYP* p. 214, we can also expect a surge in exoplanet detection by dedicated searches for dimming of starlight when a planet passes through our line of sight, and eventually by means of interferometry to obtain images and spectra of the planets themselves. As described in *TYP* p. 217, spectroscopy is likely to develop into the most promising tool we can expect to have in the coming decades for detecting (non-sentient) life, by means of its influence on a planet's atmosphere.

High spatial resolution images of exoplanets remain in the indefinite future, but we can at least use our experience of planets in our own solar system to imagine how some of them detected so far might look (Figure 14.4).

Figure 14.4 A artist's impression of the giant planet Gliese 876b (foreground) orbiting the star Gliese 876, which is of a type known as a red dwarf. By analogy with the giant planets in our own solar system, some substantial satellites have been drawn in orbit about the planet.

14.1.2 Life

TYP concludes with a discussion of the possibilities for life on planetary bodies orbiting other stars.

Question 14.1

Look at Figure 14.4 and speculate on where in this view life might occur. Use the following additional information to help you. Gliese 876 is about a hundred times less luminous than the Sun. At the orbital distance of its planet Gliese 876b, the heat received from the star is about ten times more than the solar heating at Jupiter but less than the solar heating at Mars. ◀

TYP p. 217 introduces the Drake equation as a means to estimate first the likely number of life-bearing planets in our galaxy, and then the likely number of civilizations that might be prepared to communicate with us. *TYP* describes the equation in words only. As this is a science course, I'll draw the discussion to a close by expressing the equation as a mathematical formula that you should be able to use as a basis for your own calculations.

TYP p. 216 describes in words how the number of life-bearing planets in our galaxy (which we will call N_{life}) can be estimated by the equation:

$$N_{\mathrm{life}} = R \times p_{\mathrm{s}} \times p_{\mathrm{p}} \times n \times p_{\mathrm{l}} \times T_{\mathrm{l}} \qquad (14.1)$$

in which R is the rate of star formation in our galaxy (stars per year), p_{s} is the proportion of those stars that are Sun-like, p_{p} is the proportion of Sun-like stars that have planets, n is the average number of planetary bodies round each such star capable of supporting life, p_{l} is the average probability of life arising on any planetary body capable of supporting life, and T_{l} is the length of time (in years) for which life persists once it has become established.

All the p values (which represent proportions, or fractions) must be numbers less than (or equal to) 1. Widely accepted values for R, p_{s} and p_{p} are 20 per year, 0.1 and 0.5. The value of n is likely to be at least 1 (if you accept that, in addition to the Earth, Mars and Europa are capable of supporting life, then n has a value of 3 in the Solar System). T_{l} has reached 4×10^9 years on the Earth, and if you accept that life is likely to be hard to snuff out entirely once established, then a large number like this is what we should use in the equation. The remaining value, p_{l}, is the only one that is highly controversial. For the sake of argument, let's assume that life begins on only one suitable planet in a hundred. The value of p_{l} implied by this is 0.01.

Question 14.2

Using the values listed above, use Equation 14.1 to estimate the number of life-bearing planets in our galaxy. ◀

The answer to this question suggests forty million life-bearing planetary bodies in our galaxy. Given that the values of the other terms in the equation are reasonably well-known, only likely way that the actual number of life-bearing planets could be as small as 1 (i.e., just the Earth) is if the actual value of p_{l} (the probability of life starting on any suitable world) is about forty million times less than the value of 0.01 that we used! Furthermore, for this to be valid, it would have to be totally impossible for microorganisms to survive passage from planet to planet on fragments of ejecta from impacts in the way suggested in section 7.1.

When it comes to estimating the number of planets with technologically active civilizations wishing to communicate (N_{comm}), we have to modify Equation 14.1 by inserting extra terms: p_{i} to represent the proportion of life-bearing worlds where intelligence develops and p_{c} to represent the probability of intelligent life developing the means and will to broadcast. As before, these p terms must have values less than (or equal to) 1. We also have to replace T_{l} by a smaller value T_{c} representing the lifetime of a technological civilization or (if shorter) the length of time during which it wishes to communicate. Modified in this way, we now have the standard Drake equation:

$$N_{\mathrm{comm}} = R \times p_{\mathrm{s}} \times p_{\mathrm{p}} \times n \times p_{\mathrm{l}} \times p_{\mathrm{i}} \times p_{\mathrm{c}} \times T_{\mathrm{c}} \qquad (14.2)$$

Question 14.3

TYP p. 217 suggests values of 1 and 0.5 for p_{i} and p_{c}, respectively. Use these, plus a duration of 100 years for T_{c}, to determine the average number of civilizations wishing to communicate. ◀

Using these values, the Drake equation suggests that the long-term average number of civilizations in our galaxy wishing to communicate is less than one. If true, then it is unlikely that our galaxy contains another civilization wishing to communicate at the same time as us. However, this has to be an underestimate if p_l (the probability of life starting on any suitable world) is greater than one in a hundred or if the average lifetime of technological civilizations significantly exceeds a century. If we are sensible, our civilization could last indefinitely, and if others are equally careful then N_{comm} could be a fairly large number.

Some serious commentators have argued that it may not be wise deliberately to draw attention to ourselves, in case our neighbours are hostile. However, if you wish to help the search for neighbours that wish to communicate with us, you can download a screensaver from http://setiathome.ssl.berkeley.edu/ that will use the idle time of your PC to help to search for signals hidden amongst the vast amount of data in a radio survey of the sky. Maybe in the next hundred years we will learn more about the planets of other stars by means of information beamed to us by aliens than we will by our own efforts.

14.2 Chapter 14 questions

Now try to answer the following questions, to remind you of some of the things you have learned and test your understanding of them.

Question 14.4

Which of the following techniques has not detected planets orbiting other stars?

A Dimming of starlight as the planet passes between us and the star

B Oscillation in the star's position indicated by periodic changes in wavelengths of spectral lines

C Wobble in the star's motion indicated by precise measurements of its position

D Images transmitted back to the Earth by a passing spacecraft ◀

Question 14.5

The discovery of two planets orbiting the star HD 38529 was announced in 2000. Both planets were detected simultaneously by the radial velocity method. One is about one Jupiter-mass and orbits at 0.13 AU and the other is at least 12 Jupiter-masses and orbits at 3.7 AU.

(a) What should be the official names of each of these planets?

(b) Supposing the next planet of HD 38529 to be discovered was an Earth-mass object at 0.9 AU, what should it be called? ◀

15 Revision questions and Activity

Now, to help you to prepare for the End of Course Assessment, have a go at the following questions and Activity 15.1, which are intended to help you to revise material from throughout this course. I hope you have enjoyed the course, and I wish you success with the ECA and in any other courses that you may take in the future.

Question 15.1

Which terrestrial planet is described by the following: density greater than 4 g cm^{-3}, a greenhouse effect keeping the surface warmer than it would otherwise be, strong seasonal effects on climate?

Question 15.2

Which two of the following are *least* likely to have silicate lava flows less than 500 million years old? Venus, Earth, Moon, Mars, Io, Triton.

Question 15.3

Figure 15.1 is an image recorded in visible light of a 10 km wide area of the surface of a planetary body. Solar illumination is from the left. Bearing in mind the features visible in this image, decide which of the following planetary bodies this image must be from: Mercury, Venus, Moon, Mars, Io, Europa, Ganymede, Enceladus.

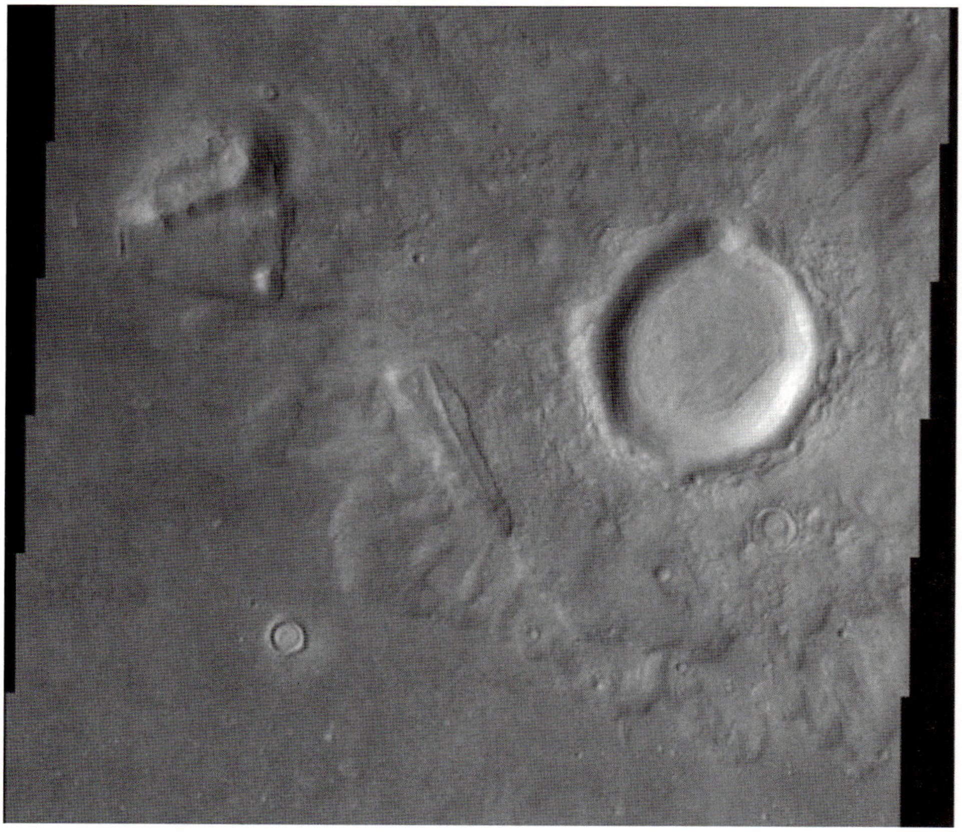

Figure 15.1 Image for use in Question 15.3.

Question 15.4

A 30 km diameter body with the provisional designation 2002 VG_{131} orbits the Sun at an average distance of 17.5 AU, with a perihelion at 14.9 AU and an aphelion at 20.1 AU. Choose from the following lists (i) the correct value for its orbital period, (ii) the date of its discovery, and (iii) the class of object to which this belongs:

(i) 6.7 years; 57.5 years; 73.2 years; 90.1 years

(ii) 1–15 April 2002; 1–15 November 2002

(iii) a Near-Earth Object; a main belt asteroid; a Jupiter Trojan asteroid; a Centaur; a classical Kuiper belt object; a Scattered Disk Object ◀

Question 15.5

Figure 15.2 is a graph of the radial velocity of a star believed to have a single massive planet in orbit around it. This graph has been corrected to remove the effects of the Earth's own orbital motion. Select from the following lists the correct statements about (i) the orientation of this planet's orbit, (ii) the shape of this planet's orbit, and (iii) its orbital period:

(i) the orbital plane could lie exactly perpendicular to our line of sight; the orbital plane could lie exactly in our line of sight

(ii) the orbit is virtually circular; the orbit has a significant eccentricity

(iii) 10 days; 23 days; 33 days; 43 days ◀

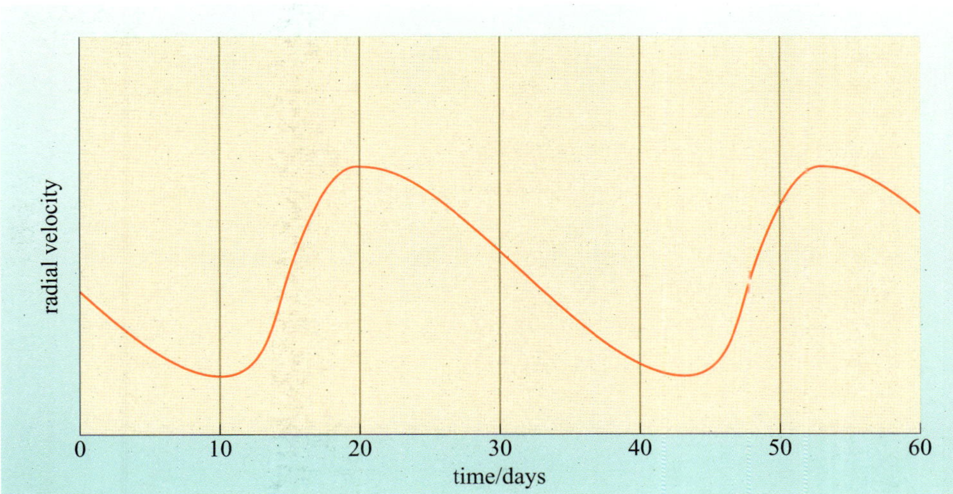

Figure 15.2 Radial velocity curve for use in Question 15.5.

Activity 15.1 Planetary science in the news

(The estimated time for this Activity is 20 minutes.)

Stories related to planetary science and space exploration often feature in the news media, whether on TV, radio, newspapers or Internet sites. Now you have reached the end of this course, I hope you will find that your increased knowledge and understanding will enable you to better appreciate the significance of any such stories that you come across. Sometimes you may be able to spot that the reporter has got something wrong, or perhaps oversimplified something (even press releases from the science teams responsible for a discovery can do this, as you saw in Question 12.2).

The following news item appeared on the BBC science Internet site in January 2003. Read it, and then answer the questions below in the light of what you have learned during this course.

> **Dancing with Neptune**
>
> Astronomers have discovered an object orbiting the Sun on a similar path to the planet Neptune. The rare body is a type of asteroid known as a Trojan. Clusters of Trojans are known to share the same orbit as Jupiter. The object, catalogued as 2001 QR_{322}, is the first to be found in association with Neptune. 'Neptunian Trojans were long suspected to exist and it is gratifying to finally know that they do,' said US team member Eugene Chiang of the University of California at Berkeley. The first Trojan associated with Jupiter was discovered in 1906 and about 1,600 such objects are now known.
>
> 2001 QR_{322} was found during a survey of the outer Solar System using telescopes in the US and Chile funded by the US space agency (NASA). It is estimated to be about 230 km (140 miles) in diameter and, like Neptune, requires about 166 years to orbit the Sun.
>
> Researchers originally found it on 21 August 2001 in deep digital images taken with the four-metre Blanco Telescope at Cerro Tololo. However, it took over a year of observations along with orbital calculations to prove that 2001 QR_{322} is a Neptune Trojan.
>
> Astronomer Eugene Chiang said: 'The orbit of 2001 QR_{322} is remarkably stable; projections of its trajectory into the future reveal that it can co-orbit with Neptune for at least billions of years. It is likely that 2001 QR_{322} is a dynamically pristine object whose orbital eccentricity and inclination have been largely unaltered by processes that afflicted the majority of bodies in the outer Solar System.'

(a) Do you think 2001 QR_{322} is most appropriately classified as an 'asteroid', as in this news item? If not, what other term(s) can you suggest?

(b) 2001 QR_{322} is described in this news item as a 'Neptunian Trojan'. If this is correct, where would you expect to find it, relative to the position of Neptune itself?

(c) The news item says that 2001 QR_{322} and Neptune each take 'about 166 years to orbit the Sun'. Do you think this value is correctly reported?

Answers to questions

Question 1.1

The correct answer is D. Uranus was discovered in 1781 (long after Galileo's death) by William Herschel. That information, plus confirmation of Galileo's achievements, is given on *TYP* pp. 3–4.

Question 1.2

The correct answer is F. Basic advice for recognizing planets by colour and possible location in the sky is given in Activity 1.3. Venus appears white, and is always fairly close to the Sun in the sky, so when the Sun is below the horizon, Venus (if visible) can only be in the west after sunset or in the east before dawn. Option A is wrong because Venus never strays far enough from the Sun to be south at midnight. Options B and D are wrong because Venus is not red. Option C is wrong because Venus, if visible after sunset, has to be in the west, not the east. Option E is incorrect, because although the object has the right colour and possible location for Venus, if we can see that it is moving over such a short period then it cannot be a planet.

Question 2.1

Only the first item in the list has been touched on so far. This reads: 'the basic layout of the Solar System, what it is made of, and how bodies move round their orbits'. However, nothing has been said yet about 'what it is made of' (in fact, this comes mostly near the end of the chapter, on pp. 19–20).

Question 2.2

We could write 150×10^6 km (because a million is 1 000 000 which is 10^6). However, it is better to make the number on the left take a value between one and ten, and write the whole thing as 1.5×10^8 km (because 150 can be written as 1.5×10^2, and $1.5 \times 10^2 \times 10^6 = 1.5 \times 10^8$; refer to Box 6.1 in the booklet *Background material on maths skills* if you are uncertain about treating powers of ten in this way).

Question 2.3

(a) We just have to multiply 1.5×10^8 km by 1000 (which is 10^3) to convert from kilometres into metres:

$$1.5 \times 10^8 \times 10^3 = 1.5 \times 10^{11},$$

so the answer is 1.5×10^{11} m.

(b) It is quoted to two significant figures, and tells us that the actual value lies closer to 1.5×10^8 km than to either 1.4×10^8 km or 1.6×10^8 km (150×10^6 km than to either 140×10^6 km or 160×10^6 km).

(c) 1.49×10^8 km would be wrong, because the actual value is closer to 1.50×10^8 km. (This shows the value of sticking as closely as possible to formal scientific notation, because we would normally assume that 150×10^6 km is quoted to two significant figures, whereas if we write 1.50×10^8 km the final zero after the decimal point is a clear indication that we mean 1.50×10^8 km (three significant figures) rather than 1.5×10^8 km (two significant figures).

Question 2.4

$$1^2 = 1 \times 1 = 1$$

$$1^3 = 1 \times 1 \times 1 = 1$$

$$2^2 = 2 \times 2 = 4$$

$$2^3 = 2 \times 2 \times 2 = 8$$

$$4^2 = 4 \times 4 = 16$$

$$4^3 = 4 \times 4 \times 4 = 64$$

$$5^2 = 5 \times 5 = 25$$

$$5^3 = 5 \times 5 \times 5 = 125$$

$$72^2 = 72 \times 72 = 5184$$

$$72^3 = 72 \times 72 \times 72 = 373\,248$$

Incidentally, the long way to work out squares on most calculators is to key in the number, press the × symbol, then key in the same number again followed by the = key. Most calculators have a 'squared' key, sometimes labelled x^2. If yours is like this, you can work out the square of a number by keying in the number and then pressing the 'squared' key. You probably wont even have to press the = key to see the result.

Few calculators have a 'cubed' key, so you may think that the only way to work out a cube is to key in 'number, ×, number, ×, number, ='. However, if your calculator has a key labelled x^y you can use this to work out cubes by keying in 'number, x^y, 3, ='. (You could also use this to work out squares by keying 'number, x^y, 2, =', but that is more long-winded than simply using the x^2 key.)

Question 2.5

(a) 5.973 698 992 has ten digits in total, so the value is expressed to ten significant figures in this case.

(b) To express the value to five significant figures, we have to lose the final five digits. However, 5.9736 would not be correct, because the precise value is closer to 5.9737, so the correct answer is 5.9737×10^{24} kg.

(c) To express the value to eight significant figures, we have to lose the final two digits. However, 5.973 6989 would not be correct, because the precise value is closer to 5.973 6990, so the correct answer is $5.973\,6990 \times 10^{24}$ kg. [Note that the final zero is important. If we left it off, and wrote $5.973\,699 \times 10^{24}$ kg instead, that would be only seven significant figures.]

Question 2.6

From Equations 2.1 and 2.2, we know that $a^3/P^2 = 1$.

This means that $a^3 = P^2$ (provided that we quote a in AU and P in years).

Table 2.1 gives a value of 0.39 AU for a, so inserting this value we can calculate

$$(0.39)^3 = 0.059\,319$$

This is the value of the value of P^2, so P is the square root of this. A calculator will show you that the square root of 0.059 319 is 0.2435. Strictly speaking, we should quote this to just two significant figures, because we have calculated it using a value of a that we were given only to two significant figures and it would be wrong to pretend that our answer can be more precise than what we started with. The answer is thus 0.24, so Mercury's orbital period is 0.24 years. [*Comment*: '0.24 years' means '0.24 Earth-years' of course. By definition, Mercury's orbital period has to be exactly one Mercury-year.]

Question 2.7

The correct answer is B. Differentiation is described on *TYP* p. 13, and is defined in the glossary.

Question 2.8

The correct answer is B. These four are all giant planets, of which the largest and most hydrogen-rich pair Jupiter and Saturn are sometimes distinguished as the gas giants. If you got this wrong then you probably need to re-read *TYP* pp. 14–17.

Question 2.9

The correct answer is C, spectroscopy, which is a technique for analysing composition (*TYP* p. 20). The others are all sources of heat, as described in *Planetary heat* (*TYP* pp. 20–21): high velocity collisions during planetary growth are the main source of primordial heat, whereas radioactive decay (radiogenic heating) and tidal heating are heat sources that continue to operate.

Question 2.10

A–D are all genuine (and correct) names. Caloris Planitia is on Mercury (you will meet it in the next chapter where it is called the Caloris basin), Nightingale Corona is on Venus (named after Florence Nightingale), Kepler is a lunar crater (remember that crater names do not include a descriptor term), and Pavonis Mons is a mountain on Mars that is thought to be a volcano. The incorrect name, which you were asked to choose, is E. A network of intersecting valleys should have the descriptor Labyrinthus, according to Table 2.1, whereas Vallis indicates a single valley. In fact there is a feature on Mars matching the description in the question, and which is named Noctis Labyrinthus. You can find this illustrated in *TYP* Figure 7.8.

Question 3.1

(a) You should recognize several impact craters in Figure 3.2 (outside the box), by virtue of their circular shape (when seen from above, as in this image, rather than obliquely) and because of the cluster of central peaks visible in the largest crater. This crater appears very similar to the large example in Figure 2.8. Having recognized craters, you should be able to use the shadows to tell you that the sunlight is coming from the right.

(b) The long feature is brightly lit on its right-hand side and shadowed on its left-hand side. Given that the illumination is from the right, this must be a ridge. A valley would have shadow on the right (i.e., on the wall facing away from the Sun) and be brightly lit on the opposite, Sun-facing, wall.

(c) There are numerous craters in this image, which I hope you can recognize as such by now. These all have shadows inside the left-hand part of their inward-facing walls. Shadows are therefore being cast from left to right, and so the sunlight is coming from the left. This is the opposite direction to the sunlight in Figure 3.2, or, more conveniently for comparison, *TYP* Figure 3.4. If the topography in either of these looks 'inverted' to you, try turning the book round.

Question 3.2

As described on *TYP* p. 25, Mercury is never very far from the Sun in the sky, even when at maximum elongation. It is also smaller and has a lower albedo than Venus, and so is less bright and usually hidden by the Sun's glare. Good opportunities to see Mercury are rare, and in fact I have only managed to see it myself on a few occasions.

Question 3.3

There are considerably more craters per unit area in *TYP* Figure 3.5 than in *TYP* Figure 3.4. The surface in Figure 3.5 is therefore the older of the two. The area in Figure 3.4 has been resurfaced (the text suggests by lava flows), which obliterated (presumably, buried) the older craters so that only those craters that were formed after the resurfacing event can be seen. Note that this does not mean that all the individual craters in Figure 3.5 are older than those in Figure 3.4.

Question 3.4

The incorrect statements, which are therefore the options you should have selected, are C and D. The scarp of Santa Maria Rupes is likely to reflect contraction, not expansion, of the globe. Although Mercury's day is twice as long as its year, its rotation period is actually shorter than its year; Section 3.1.1 explains this.

Question 3.5

There are several impact craters visible in this image. They all have bright illumination on the parts of their inner walls that face towards the top right, whereas the opposite part of their inner walls (facing towards the lower left) are in shadow. The illumination must be coming from the upper right.

Question 3.6

The incorrect statements are B and E. The main crater has a central peak and terracing on its wall, and is clearly not bowl-shaped (unlike the younger 20 km diameter just inside its northeast rim). Many of the small <5 km craters outside the main crater are secondary craters (the caption tells you this), but no rays are visible. In fact, rays, if they are present, can usually be seen only on images recorded when the Sun was high in the sky. On this image there are plenty of shadows, so the illumination is not suitable for revealing rays.

Question 4.1

As described in *The interior* (*TYP* p. 42), Venus is thought to have a core. Part of this may be an electrically conducting fluid, but the planet's rotation is too slow to stir this up into the motion necessary to generate a magnetic field (there is summary of magnetic field generation in the second bullet point in Section 3.1.2). The correct answer is B. The temperature would be relevant only if the question was about a possible remanent magnetic field, but in fact it asks about generation of a field.

Question 4.2

As described in Section 4.1, a gas must consist of molecules containing at least two atoms of different elements in order to be a strong absorber of infrared radiation and thereby trap heat. Carbon dioxide, water vapour, and sulfur dioxide (chemical formula SO_2) all match this criterion. On the other hand nitrogen and argon each contain only one element, and so cannot be greenhouse gases. Section 4.1 tells you that nitrogen gas consists of molecules made of two nitrogen atoms (N_2), and in fact argon is an unreactive element that does not even bond with itself and consists simply of single atoms.

Question 4.3

It is a pretty simple concept really – it just means escape of gases through volcanoes, which is more or less what is said on *TYP* p. 20. [*Comment*: As explained on *TYP* pp. 14–16, a planet of less than about ten Earth-masses won't have had strong enough gravity to scavenge gas directly from the solar nebula. The atmospheres of Venus, the Earth and Mars are believed to have originated by the subsequent escape of gases that had become trapped in the planets' interiors as they grew.]

Question 4.4

(a) The western rim of the western dome is bright, and the eastern rims of both domes are dark (as if in partial shadow). This indicates radar illumination from the west (i.e. from the left).

(b) The flat tops of the domes and the flat terrain beyond the domes both appear a similar mid-grey tone, and so the surface roughness must be similar everywhere. Note, however, the fine bright lines indicating surface fractures that show a different pattern on the domes and on the surrounding terrain, so that the previous comment about similar roughness applies only to the areas of surface between fractures.

Question 4.5

(a) The pale area in the west is a series of overlapping lava flows, which you can deduce from the elongated lobate (i.e., lobe-like) shapes and by comparison with *TYP* Figure 4.4. These lava flows appear bright on radar, and so their surfaces must be rough.

(b) In the east there are several patches of intensely fractured high ground jutting out above much darker (i.e., much smoother) lowland. These are examples of tessera terrain, as illustrated in the left-hand part of *TYP* Figure 4.5. A more extensive version of this image appears on the S196 CD-ROM as Venus31.

Question 4.6

As stated in the discussion of Figure 4.8 on *TYP* p. 49, it is very unlikely that liquid water can have occurred after the present surface was formed. Instead, the channels were probably cut by flowing lava. As described on *TYP* p. 52, the favoured way to explain the relatively uniform (about 500 million years) age of the surface is that a proportion of the internally generated heat is being trapped below the lithosphere, so that this part of the mantle must indeed be getting warmer. Option B is therefore the one you should have chosen. C is incorrect; *TYP* Figure 4.10 and the images of well-formed craters you saw in Activity 4.1 show that craters generally have rough, radar-bright ejecta surrounding their rims. D is incorrect; there is no discernible difference in crater abundance between terrain types, and this is why it is believed that Venus experienced global resurfacing (probably about 500 million years ago).

Question 5.1

Both A and D are results of rapid rotation, as discussed on *TYP* pp. 57–58. Refer back to Section 5.1.1 if you are in any doubt that the Earth's day-length (B) is a result of rapid rotation. The Earth's magnetic field is very strong (*TYP* p. 60) and *TYP* p. 42 states that Venus's magnetic field has to be much weaker than the Earth's because Venus rotates so slowly, so E is a correct consequence too. You should have chosen C; no one knows why the Earth has plate tectonics whereas Venus (apparently) does not, however there is no suggestion in *TYP* that this difference can be explained by the rate of planetary rotation.

Question 5.2

A is a common misconception, but is quite wrong. The crust and the uppermost mantle form a single mechanical unit called the lithosphere (*TYP* p. 13), and the crust is firmly welded to the part of the mantle upon which it sits. The plates illustrated in *TYP* Figure 5.4 consist of the full thickness of the lithosphere moving over the weaker asthenosphere part of the mantle. B is incorrect, because volcanoes like Hawaii sit above deep-seated mantle plumes that are unrelated to plate boundaries. C is incorrect: as described on *TYP* p. 61 oceanic crust is a result of melting within the mantle. The same paragraph shows that D is incorrect too. E is correct, as demonstrated by the inability of some kinds of seismic waves to travel through the outer part of the core (*TYP* p. 60).

Question 5.3

As described on *TYP* pp. 56–57, plant life has removed most of the original carbon dioxide, some of which has been broken down to liberate oxygen, which was originally not present (as a free species) at all. A (very) small proportion of this oxygen has been turned into ozone. Recent human-induced changes to the atmosphere include release of additional carbon dioxide (from burning fossil fuels) and methane (from agriculture).

Question 6.1

The Moon's atmospheric pressure is quoted as 2×10^{-14}, relative to Earth, whereas Mercury's is 10^{-15}. Thus, the Moon's atmospheric pressure relative to Mercury's is $2 \times 10^{-14}/10^{-15} = 2 \times 10^{1} = 20$. This is closer to ten than to a hundred, so we would say that the Moon's atmospheric pressure is one order of magnitude greater than Mercury's.

Question 6.2

You might have picked temperature, on the grounds that lava will solidify quicker on a colder body. However, the Moon's average surface temperature is not much lower than the Earth's, so this is not actually the principal factor. The big difference between the two bodies is surface gravity. The Moon's surface gravity is only 0.17 (about a sixth) of the Earth's. This means that the force acting to spread flowing lava away from its source is six times weaker on the Moon than on the Earth. Lunar lava flows should thus tend to be thicker than equivalent flows on Earth. [*Comment*: This may be one of the reasons why lava tubes on the Moon have been able to attain much bigger dimensions than lava tubes on the Earth.]

Question 6.3

A is incorrect; 70 km is the average thickness of the crust (*TYP* p. 70), not of the lithosphere – the base of which is quoted as 'about 1000 km' on the same page. B is incorrect; 1290 km is the minimum likely *depth* to the top of the core (*TYP* p. 66). C is correct, as demonstrated by crater densities and from samples dated using natural radioactivity (*TYP* pp. 72–73). D is incorrect; the maria are basins that were flooded by lava (*TYP* p. 73), which is still there (even though it has long since solidified). E is incorrect; the third paragraph of *TYP* p. 66 gives reasons for supposing that the whole of the Moon's core is now solid.

Question 7.1

The incorrect name, which you were asked to identify, is A. Planum should be used as a descriptor term for a plateau or high plain. Hellas is an impact basin and so is low-lying, and its formal name is Hellas Planitia, in which planitia is the correct descriptor term for a low plain. Thus Hellas Planitia and Isidis Planitia use the same descriptor term consistently to denote comparable features. Vastitas Borealis is the true formal name of the northern lowlands, and uses vastitas as the descriptor term for an extensive plain (borealis means northern; note that there is no rule that the descriptor term has to come after the rest of the name, though it usually does). Alba Patera is a correct name. You may have seen it in Mars20; but in any case Table 2.1 shows that patera is an appropriate descriptor term for an irregular, often scalloped-edged, crater. In practice, those volcanoes on Mars with particularly gentle slopes tend to be given the descriptor term relating to their summit crater, whereas mons (meaning mountain) is reserved for steeper volcanoes. Abalos Undae is a genuine name for a dune field, using the descriptor undae, and the dunes shown in Mars55 are in fact part of this field.

Question 7.2

The tilt of Mars's axis varies between 5° and 35°, and this greatly influences the climate especially in polar regions (*TYP* p. 92). As described on *TYP* p. 56, the Earth's climate is affected by a similar process but the range of axial inclination is much less.

Question 7.3

The feature in the centre of *TYP* Figure 7.5 is an impact crater, with an obvious central peak. This peak and the part of inner crater wall that faces left both cast shadows to the left, whereas the right side of the peak and the right-facing part of the inner crater wall are brightly illuminated, so the sunlight must be coming from the right. This interpretation is consistent with the appearance of the lobe-like margin to this ejecta blanket of this rather special kind of crater. The ejecta blanket is sufficiently thick that its margin casts a shadow to where it faces to the left.

In Figure 7.6 (left) both channel systems show shadows cast by the left-facing walls and brightly-lit right-facing walls. The impact craters show a similar pattern, so in this image too the sunlight must be coming from the right. However in Figure 7.6 (right) the pattern of light and shade in the channel is reversed, so in this case the sunlight must be coming from the left.

[*Comment*: If you are still having trouble visualizing illumination direction, please look at *TYP* Figure 7.3. In this case the caption tells you that the illumination is from the right. However, even with this information, some people find it hard to visualise the terrain correctly, and they 'see' the craters as flat-topped circular hills and the valleys as ridges. If this happens to you, try turning the page upside down, as suggested in Box 2.5. This may help your visualization to fall into place.]

Question 7.4

There are a few impact craters on the lava flow that occupies the upper part of the image, though they are hard to distinguish among the irregular texture of the lava surface. Impact craters are more common and easier to see in the bottom third of the image, which shows an older surface that has been buried by the lava flow in the rest of the image. These are simple bowl-shaped craters without central peaks, which is what you should expect given their small size (the image is 1.5 km wide, so the largest crater is less than 100 m across). Some of the craters, such as the large one in the lower left, appear to be partly buried by sediment. A 20 m diameter crater in the lower right has what looks like a lobate ejecta blanket that is similar (though on a much smaller scale) to the one around the crater in *TYP* Figure 7.5, and may indicate impact into ice-rich ground.

The insides of craters have shade within their top left halves whereas the parts of their inner walls that face towards the top left are brightly illuminated. The most prominent shadow cast by the steep edge to the lava flow occurs where this slope faces towards the lower right, and shadows cast by presumed upward-projecting knobs on the lava flow also lie on their lower right. All these indications suggest sunlight coming from the upper left.

Question 8.1

(a) (i) The 3 : 2 resonance is (11.86 years × 2)/3 = (23.72 years)/3 = 7.91 years. (ii) The 7 : 2 resonance is (11.86 years × 2)/7 = (23.72 years)/7 = 3.39 years

(b) There is nothing in Table 8.1 with a period close to 7.91 years, but Gaspra (3.28 years) is close to the 3.39 year 7 : 2 resonance but slightly shorter. Braille (3.58 years) and Vesta (3.63 years) have periods almost as close, but slightly longer.

Question 8.2

(a) 1994 X means 1–15 December 1994. M is the 12th letter (after discounting I), so M_1 indicates 12 + 25, which is 37. 1994 XM_1 was therefore the 37th object discovered in the period 1–15 December 1994.

(b) 2000 W means 16–30 November 2000. O is the 14th letter (after discounting I), so O_{107} indicates 14 + (107 × 25), which is 14 + 2675 = 2689. 2000 WO_{14} was therefore the 2689th object discovered in the period 16–30 November 2000.

Question 8.3

Even the largest asteroid is too small to have pulled itself into a near-spherical shape (see Section 2.2.4). Another reason that you may have thought of is that they do not fit the Section 2.2.4 criterion of being considerably larger than any other object in the same region of space, which is met by all eight of the obvious planets. For example, the largest and second largest asteroids (Ceres and Pallas) orbit the Sun at almost the same distance, but the diameter of Ceres is less than twice that of Pallas (*TYP* Table 8.1).

Question 8.4

A is untrue; most determined densities are too low to be solid rock (see *TYP* p. 103). B is untrue; *TYP* p. 101 states that colour type (and hence composition) correlates with distance from the Sun (and hence orbital period). *TYP* pp. 103–104 show that C is untrue. D is correct; 5.93 years is half Jupiter's orbital period, and *TYP* p. 98 states that the 2 : 1 orbital resonance is one of the virtually unoccupied Kirkwood gaps. E is untrue; *TYP* p. 98 states that all known asteroids have prograde orbits.

Question 8.5

According to the rules in Table 8.1, 16–31 March 2010 would determine that the provisional designation would begin 2010 F. To get the rest of the code, we need to determine how many times we can divide 210 by 25. The answer is 8, with the remainder 10. The 10 means that the second letter of the code is the tenth letter in the sequence A–Z with I omitted, which is K. The 8 becomes the subscript, so the complete provisional designation would be 2010 FK_8.

Question 8.6

$a^3 = P^2$ (provided that we quote a in AU and P in years), so in this case:

$$(2.78)^3 = 21.48 = P^2$$

The value of P is thus the square root of 21.48, which, as a calculator will show you, is 4.64 (quoting to the same number of significant figures as the value we started with). Eugenia's orbital period is thus 4.64 years.

Question 9.1

(a) Jupiter has four Hadley cells in each hemisphere between the equator and the pole. The Earth has only three (*TYP* Figure 5.1), Venus has only one per hemisphere, and Mars has an even simpler pattern with a single dominant cell rising at the sub-solar latitude and flowing across the equator towards the pole in the opposite hemisphere. The differences among the terrestrial planets are caused by Venus's very slow rotation, and the lack of oceans to even out solar heating on Mars. Jupiter's extra cell relative to the Earth is primarily because Jupiter rotates much faster than the Earth, which restricts how far a parcel of atmosphere can travel in a north–south direction before being deflected sideways into zonal (east–west) winds.

(b) Other differences are that Jupiter's atmosphere receives more energy from the planet's interior than from the Sun, and that it is much deeper, with no clearly defined base. The chemistry is different too: Jupiter's atmosphere is almost entirely hydrogen and helium (similar to the Sun) coloured with traces of hydrogen-bearing compounds, whereas the carbon dioxide and nitrogen common to all three main terrestrial planets occur in insignificant proportions. [*Comment*: This difference is because the atmospheres of the terrestrial planets originated by gas escaping from the rocky interior (*TYP* p. 20), whereas the atmospheres of the giant planets were captured directly from the solar nebula, thanks to these planets' much stronger gravity (*TYP* p. 16).]

Question 9.2

According to *TYP* p. 113, at depths greater than about 10 000 km, Jupiter consists mostly of hydrogen having the properties of a molten metal, described as 'metallic hydrogen'. This zone continues much deeper than 12 000 km (see *TYP* Figure 2.5), and at 12 000 km we can infer from *TYP* p. 113 that the pressure must be greater than a million times the Earth's sea-level atmospheric pressure, and the temperature must be greater than 6000 °C (which are the values quoted for 10 000 km depth).

Question 9.3

The correct sequence is (b), (c), (a), (d), although there may be local exceptions. Generally, ball of string texture is the oldest. Several generations of larger ridges can be seen cutting across (overprinting) the finer scale ball-of-string texture, so these larger ridges must be younger. Ball of string texture and some of the larger ridges are both disrupted into chaos, notably in the large area of Conamara chaos in the left (see *TYP* Plate 9) but also in smaller chaos regions that cut across some of the large ridge systems in the lower right, so chaos generation is younger than ridge generation. Distribution of the ejecta patches is probably the last event, because the splashes of white can be seen even on the re-frozen matrix between the chaos rafts (most clearly seen in the lower left of *TYP* Plate 9).

Question 9.4

TYP p. 128 quotes Io's heat loss as 2.5 watts per square metre and the Earth's as 0.08 watts per square metre. Dividing these two numbers we get 2.5/0.08 = 250/8 = 31.25.

This is closer to 10 than to 100, so Io's rate of heat loss per square metre is approximately one order of magnitude greater than the Earth's.

Question 9.5

Io does indeed orbit within a zone of magnetically confined radiation (e.g., CD-ROM Jupiter6) but this is not the origin of the heat that powers Io's volcanoes. The correct answer is B (*TYP* p. 124).

Question 9.6

Both are believed to have a dense, iron-rich core surrounded by a rocky mantle, which is the key characteristic of terrestrial planets according to *TYP* p. 13 and the Glossary. In terms of size and density they are both similar to the Moon, which is often regarded as a terrestrial planet. The composition of Io's volcanic surface is likely to be sufficiently different from its mantle to be regarded as a distinct crust, which is another feature of terrestrial planets. Europa has about 100 km of ice (or ice + water) hiding its rocky part; this thickness is only a small fraction of the global radius, and in this respect Europa is transitional between a 'normal' terrestrial planet and a large icy body, such as Ganymede, in which the ice is much thicker.

Question 9.7

A, C and D are all believed likely to happen, although C is described in *TYP* only for Europa. B is impossible, because tholins are tarry substances and therefore require carbon (Section 9.1.5), which is not present in a molecule of water (H_2O). [*Comment*: The tholins that may contribute to radiation-darkening of Ganymede's ice could originate from the action of radiation on carbon dioxide ice.]

Question 9.8

(a) These features are rather too small for you to make out their nature on this Figure, but the only kinds of feature that are given names without a descriptor term are (impact) craters and eruptive centres. There are no signs of eruption here, and in fact these are impact craters.

(b) According to Table 2.1 'sulcus' is a descriptor term meaning parallel (or nearly parallel) ridges and furrows.

(c) The map shows belts of pale terrain cutting through dark terrain. This is a characteristic feature of Ganymede, and the identification is backed up by the abundance of impact craters (few of them actually named) on both terrain types. The sulci are belts of pale terrain that cut through dark terrain, and 'nearly parallel ridges and furrows' is a fair description of the visual appearance of Ganymede's pale terrain. Nippur Sulcus, near the northeast (top right) corner of the map, is in fact the belt of pale terrain that runs diagonally across *TYP* Figure 9.17. That figure also shows Akitu Sulcus, the tapering belt of pale terrain that extends westwards from Nippur Sulcus.

Question 10.1

Both planets have strong magnetic fields, but Saturn's is exactly aligned with the planet's axis of rotation (*TYP* p. 143), so one correct answer is B. Saturn's rings are mostly metre-sized chunks of ice (*TYP* p. 147), not low-albedo dust like Jupiter's, so the other correct answer is E. All the other properties are shared by both planets.

Question 10.2

The ratio between the orbital periods of Enceladus and Mimas is 1.370 : 0.942 = 1.454 : 1 = 2.91 : 2. According to Box 9.2, this is too far from an exact ratio of whole numbers (such as 3 : 2) to count as orbital resonance for tidal heating purposes. The ratio of the orbital periods of Tethys and Mimas is 1.888 : 0.942 = 2.00 : 1, which is an exact 2 : 1 resonance. According to Box 9.2 this would be expected to lead to tidal heating. However, as can be seen from images of Mimas, any such tidal heating within Mimas has had no significant effects on the surface, because the heavily cratered nature of the surface does not appear to have been overprinted in any way. [*Comments*: (i) Even when orbital resonance is exact, significant tidal heating will be absent unless various other conditions are satisfied. (ii) The ratio between the orbital periods of Mimas and either Epimetheus or Janus is 0.942 : 0.695 = 1.36, which is very close to a 4 : 3 resonance (1.33). Epimetheus and Janus are both small objects incapable of contributing much to any tidal heating of Mimas, but this resonance is another example of the complex mutual interactions within satellite families.]

Question 10.3

C is correct; Titan's dense atmosphere shields the surface from radiation that could break water molecules apart, and it is too cold for ice to evaporate (*TYP* p. 160). A is wrong, because we expect water ice (H_2O, which contains oxygen) to be present at the surface. There is no suggestion in *TYP* that B is correct, and in any case we expect most of Titan's rock to be deep in its interior. D is pure fantasy.

Question 10.4

From least to most the correct order is Rhea, Tethys, Dione, Enceladus. Note that *TYP* p. 157 states 'Tethys shows fewer signs of past activity than Dione'.

Question 10.5

According to Table 2.1 'chasma' means a deep, elongated, steep-sided depression. This is a perfectly good description of how this particular feature looks.

Question 11.1

Out of this long list, only B (a strong magnetic field inclined to the planets axis) is common to the two planets. The pressure in Uranus's interior is too low to compress hydrogen into the metallic state, no phosphine has been detected, there are certainly clouds but no indications of rotating storms (although this may change when the axis of rotation is oriented sideways relative to the Sun), most of the rings are boulders rather than dust, and no orbital resonances are apparent from inspection of *TYP* Table 11.1. Uranus's visible cloud layer is methane rather than ammonia as at Jupiter (*TYP* p. 167).

Question 11.2

The dust becomes apparent by looking through the rings towards the Sun, as in *TYP* Figure 11.4. Observation of dust in rings when seen like this in so-called forward-scattered light was described in the case of Jupiter on *TYP* p. 120.

Question 11.3

On the basis of the information so far provided to you, either 'chasma' or 'vallis' would do. However, in practice, 'vallis' tends to be reserved for narrower, winding valleys and especially those with tributaries. The official name of this feature is therefore Korrigan Chasma.

Question 11.4

This is tricky, because no matter how carefully you look you can find no definite evidence that one cuts across the other. You should not worry if you were unable to make your mind up, because there is no consensus amongst the experts either. All that is clear on the image is that Korrigan Chasma is a straight trough and that Kra Chasma consists of lengths of straight trough that are offset from one another either side of Korrigan Chasma. One theory is that Kra Chasma is the older, and was originally a single straight trough whose two halves became displaced by sideways motion along the length of the younger Korrigan Chasma. An opposing theory is that Korrigan Chasma formed first, and that when Kra Chasma was created the presence of Korrigan Chasma deflected the new fractures so that Kra Chasma was born with a kink. To decide between these theories we really need higher resolution images, especially of the rather interesting area just to the left of Y on Figure 11.4, where it appears that Kra Chasma takes a few sideways steps before running into Korrigan Chasma.

Question 12.1

The only incorrect statement is C. The topmost continuous cloud layer on both planets is methane, whereas ammonia clouds are the upper layer on Jupiter and Saturn. Although it is correct that Voyager images of Neptune showed much more structure than Voyager images of Uranus (E), Hubble Space Telescope images have subsequently shown that Uranus's previously bland appearance has altered to become more Neptune-like.

Question 12.2

Within this course I have been careful to distinguish true gas giants (Jupiter and Saturn) from giant planets in general. If Uranus is a giant planet but not strictly a gas giant (Section 11.1.1) then the same applies to Neptune. However, the term 'gas giant' is excusable in the context of this press release, which does not seek to draw any distinctions between types of giant planet and is intended for reporters and the general public, who are likely to have only minimal background knowledge.

Question 12.3

Both satellites exhibit a wide range of ages of resurfaced areas, demonstrated by variations in impact crater density and probable cryovolcanic features. The only observed geysers are on Triton, although some kind of recent cryovolcanic explosive activity on Enceladus would be one way to keep Saturn's E-ring supplied with particles. Cantaloupe terrain has been recognized nowhere other than on Triton. Images of both satellites in the course materials show plenty of impact craters, though neither has a particularly densely cratered surface. There is plenty of nitrogen ice on Triton, especially in its south polar cap, but Enceladus is too warm. Tidal heating may occur on Enceladus today, but there is no known mechanism to cause tidal heating in Triton at present. Thus, from the list, B, C and E occur on Triton but not on Enceladus (A and D occur on both, F may occur on Enceladus but not on Triton).

Question 12.4

These are ridges with furrows running along them. The only suitable descriptor term in Table 2.1 is sulcus ('parallel or or nearly parallel ridges and furrows'), which you previously met on Ganymede as a descriptor term for the belts of ridged and furrowed pale terrain (Question 9.8). For no obvious reason, only the plural version is used on Triton, so the full names of these features are Slidr Sulci and Tano Sulci.

Question 12.5

Sublimation is discussed in Box 7.1. From this you should deduce that the reason why Triton's nitrogen ice sublimes rather than melts is that the pressure of nitrogen gas in Triton's atmosphere is too low to allow liquid nitrogen to exist in a stable form. [*Comment*: Sublimation of nitrogen *below* the polar cap is the most likely explanation for Triton's 'geysers'.]

Question 13.1

TYP Table 13.2 lists several other double objects in the Kuiper belt, so A is incorrect. Charon has no detected atmosphere, so B is incorrect. Charon's orbital eccentricity is quoted in the text (p. 201) as 0.002, so C is incorrect (The *Planetary facts* table on p. 199 quotes the wrong value.). D is incorrect, as comparison of *TYP* Table 12.2 and the Chapter 13 *Planetary facts* table shows. E is the only correct statement: Charon's slightly elliptical orbit must lead to some tidal heating (*TYP* p. 201) and its orbital inclination could contribute to solar tidal heating (*TYP* p. 206). [*Comment*: Both factors could also contribute to a smaller amount of tidal heating within Pluto.]

Question 13.2

Kuiper belt objects share the same provisional designation system as asteroids. If you refer to Table 8.1 you will see that Q indicates discovery in the period 16–31 August, and 1992 shows the year. B_1 indicates that this was the 27th (2 + 25) discovery during that period. Because we do not know how many other discoveries were made within the period we cannot narrow down our estimate of the date any more precisely from this designation; in fact, the first observation of this object was on 30 August.

Question 13.3

The large mean distance from the Sun (and hence long orbital period) alone should suggest to you that this is a Scattered Disk Object. This is confirmed by the high eccentricity of the orbit and supported by the significant orbital inclination.

Question 14.1

Gliese 876b is a giant planet, and given that its mass exceeds Jupiter's it is likely to be a gas giant. We know of no life that could exist in the atmosphere of such a world, though the possibility cannot be ruled out entirely. However, the speculated satellites of this giant planet would seem to be more promising. Their surfaces would be colder than that of Mars, unless boosted either by a powerful greenhouse effect caused by a dense atmosphere or by heat radiated from the planet itself, so flourishing complex life of kinds familiar on the Earth is unlikely. However, if any of these satellites is an icy body then even if it has no atmosphere, life could exist on the floor of an ice-capped ocean, thanks to heat produced either by radioactive decay or by tidal interaction with a fellow satellite.

Question 14.2

Inserting values into Equation 14.1, we get

$$N_{\text{life}} = 20 \times 0.1 \times 0.5 \times 1 \times 0.01 \times 4 \times 10^9 = 4 \times 10^7$$

Question 14.3

Inserting values into Equation 14.2, we get

$$N_{\text{comm}} = 20 \times 0.1 \times 0.5 \times 1 \times 0.01 \times 1 \times 0.5 \times 100 = 0.5$$

Question 14.4

D has not been attempted (the most distant spacecraft, Voyager 1, is less than 100 AU from the Sun, which is less than 0.1% of the distance to the nearest star. However, all three of the others have been achieved, with B (the radial velocity method) having been the most fruitful.

Question 14.5

(a) According to the rules described in Box 14.1, the inner one should be called HD 38529b and the outer one should be called HD 38529c.

(b) As the third planet to be discovered it would take the letter 'd', and be named HD 38529d. The size of its orbit is not relevant (unless discovered simultaneously with another planet of the same star).

Question 15.1

The high density rules out Mars and the Moon (and Io, if you count that as a terrestrial planet). The greenhouse effect requires a substantial atmosphere, which rules out Mercury. Only Venus and Earth are left, but Venus's axial tilt of 177.4° (retrograde but only 0.6° away from being exactly perpendicular to its orbital plane) means that seasons must be negligible. The answer is Earth. [*Comment*: you should have consulted the *Planetary facts* tables at the start of the relevant chapters for information on density and axial tilt.]

Question 15.2

Earth and Io have silicate lava flows active today. Venus was resurfaced about 500 million years ago, and the youngest flows such as in *TYP* Figure 4.4 must be younger than this. The most recent eruptions of Olympus Mons on Mars may be only a few tens of millions of years old. However, lunar volcanism ceased about a billion years (or longer) ago, and all the flows on Triton (however old they may be) are cryovolcanic rather than silicate. The correct answers are therefore the Moon and Triton.

Question 15.3

There are several impact craters in this image, though by Solar System standards the surface is fairly sparsely cratered. The largest crater (2.5 km diameter) is surrounded by a lobate ejecta blanket. This is a smaller-scale version of the martian crater Yuty that was illustrated in *TYP* Figure 7.5, whose morphology is generally taken to be evidence of water in the subsoil. The only comparable lobate ejecta blankets you have met are some on Venus, such as *TYP* Figure 4.10 (attributed to dense atmosphere), but the question tells you that Figure 15.1 was recorded in visible light. It therefore cannot be a radar image, so it has to show part of Mars rather than Venus.

Question 15.4

(i) Calculating the orbital period about the Sun is just a matter of applying Kepler's third law as in Question 2.6. You need to use the average distance from the Sun, rather than the perihelion distance or the aphelion distance (as noted in Section 2.1.2 the average distance is half the sum of the perihelion distance plus the aphelion distance). Using $a^3 = P^2$ (provided that we quote a in AU and P in years) and inserting 17.5 AU for a, we find $17.5^3 = 5359.4 = P^2$, so P (in years) is the square root of 5359.4, which is 73.208. The correct answer, expressed to an appropriate number of significant figures, is 73.2 years.

(ii) In the provisional designation, 2002 V indicates 1–15 November 2002 (and G_{131} indicates its sequence of discovery within that period); see Table 8.1.

(iii) Every point of this body's orbit is beyond that of Saturn but within that of Uranus, so it is a fairly ordinary Centaur.

Question 15.5

(i) If the planet's orbit were perpendicular to our line of sight, this would cause no wobble towards or away from the Earth, and hence no variation in radial velocity. Figure 15.2 shows periodic variation in radial velocity, so the orbital plane cannot be exactly perpendicular to our line of sight. On the other hand, the orbital plane could be exactly in our line of sight, though statistically it is more likely to be somewhat inclined.

(ii) The asymmetry of radial velocity curve, in contrast to the 51 Pegasi radial velocity curve in Figure 14.2, shows that the orbit is significantly eccentric.

(iii) The orbital period, which can most simply be measured by the time between successive peaks or between successive troughs, is 33 days.

Discussion of Activities

Activity 1.1

In the third paragraph of *TYP* p. 2, the main point is that planets and their larger satellites have been 'revealed in stunning detail by spaceprobes'. So that phrase, and sufficient previous words to pick out 'planets' and 'satellites' certainly deserve highlighting. I think it is probably worth also highlighting the phrase 'dozens of worlds' as a reminder of how many objects we will be dealing with in the course. The rest of the final sentence looks pretty important too, and maybe you highlighted this as well. My own inclination is not to, because the more you highlight, the less valuable it becomes. A rule of thumb is never to highlight more than half of a paragraph (if the whole of a paragraph is very important, then it's a good idea to draw a vertical highlight in the margin rather than tracing over each line of text).

In the fourth paragraph I decided to highlight phrases that identify the main purpose of the book, and also the distinction between planetary scientists as opposed to astronomers.

Figure A1 shows my highlighting of the both paragraphs. I hope you will agree that I have picked out the main points. There are other ways of doing this, and I would be very surprised if your highlighting was exactly the same as mine. Remember that your highlighting is for *your* benefit, so provided you are satisfied that you have picked things out that will suit your specific needs then you do not need to match my specific suggestions.

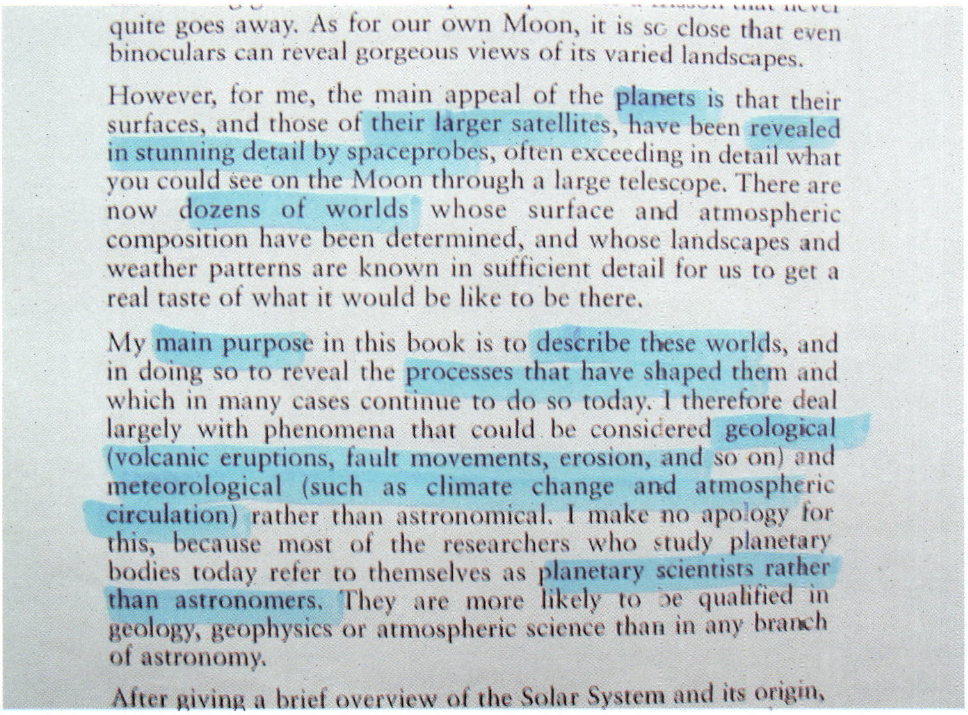
quite goes away. As for our own Moon, it is so close that even binoculars can reveal gorgeous views of its varied landscapes.

However, for me, the main appeal of the planets is that their surfaces, and those of their larger satellites, have been revealed in stunning detail by spaceprobes, often exceeding in detail what you could see on the Moon through a large telescope. There are now dozens of worlds whose surface and atmospheric composition have been determined, and whose landscapes and weather patterns are known in sufficient detail for us to get a real taste of what it would be like to be there.

My main purpose in this book is to describe these worlds, and in doing so to reveal the processes that have shaped them and which in many cases continue to do so today. I therefore deal largely with phenomena that could be considered geological (volcanic eruptions, fault movements, erosion, and so on) and meteorological (such as climate change and atmospheric circulation) rather than astronomical. I make no apology for this, because most of the researchers who study planetary bodies today refer to themselves as planetary scientists rather than astronomers. They are more likely to be qualified in geology, geophysics or atmospheric science than in any branch of astronomy.

After giving a brief overview of the Solar System and its origin,

Figure A1 An example of highlighting key parts of the text on *TYP* p. 2.

In the first paragraph of *History of the planets* I decided that the most important information was how many planets were known in the ancient world, what their names are, and what property of their appearance in the sky made them seem special. As a result, I highlighted the bits shown in Figure A2. As before, it doesn't much matter if your highlighting is a bit different to mine, provided you have identified the gist of the discussion.

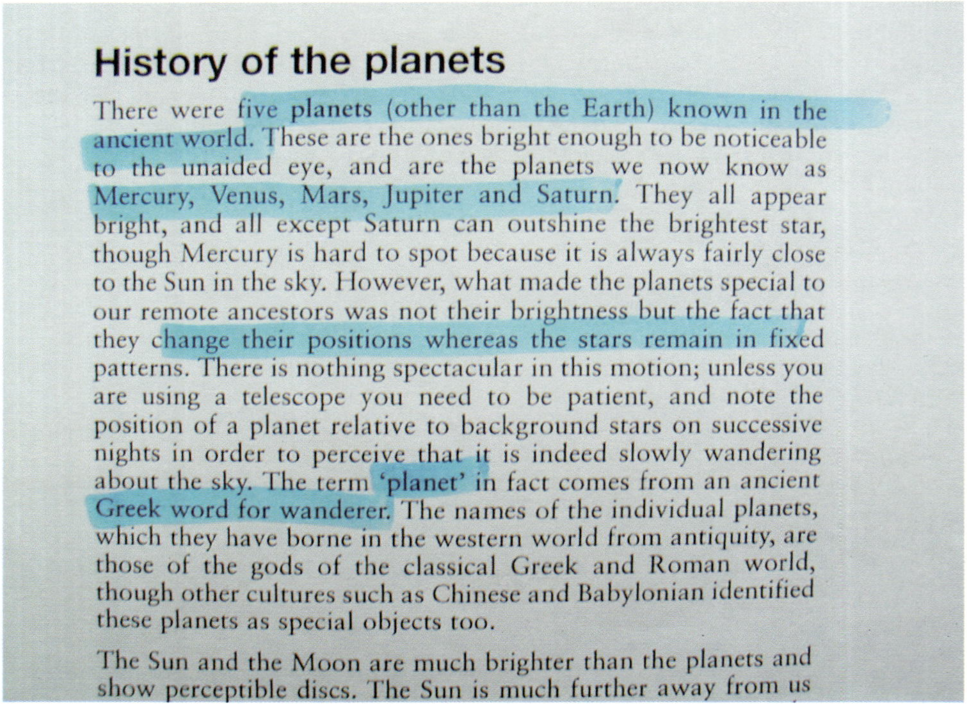

History of the planets

There were five **planets** (other than the Earth) known in the ancient world. These are the ones bright enough to be noticeable to the unaided eye, and are the planets we now know as Mercury, Venus, Mars, Jupiter and Saturn. They all appear bright, and all except Saturn can outshine the brightest star, though Mercury is hard to spot because it is always fairly close to the Sun in the sky. However, what made the planets special to our remote ancestors was not their brightness but the fact that they change their positions whereas the stars remain in fixed patterns. There is nothing spectacular in this motion; unless you are using a telescope you need to be patient, and note the position of a planet relative to background stars on successive nights in order to perceive that it is indeed slowly wandering about the sky. The term 'planet' in fact comes from an ancient Greek word for wanderer. The names of the individual planets, which they have borne in the western world from antiquity, are those of the gods of the classical Greek and Roman world, though other cultures such as Chinese and Babylonian identified these planets as special objects too.

The Sun and the Moon are much brighter than the planets and show perceptible discs. The Sun is much further away from us

Figure A2 An example of highlighting key parts of the text on *TYP* p. 3.

As well as highlighting *TYP*, you may find it helpful to highlight words or phrases in this book too. Unlike *TYP* this book has a wide margin, which is useful space for writing short notes to yourself. Examples might be 'good point!' if I've said something that strikes you as particularly valuable or 'why?' beside something that has confused you. In that case, if you subsequently get your problem sorted out you can add a brief explanation or a reference to a page in this book or in *TYP* where an explanation occurs.

Finally, you may have noticed that the word **planets** appears in bold typeface in the first sentence of *History of the planets*. As described at the top of the same page, this draws attention to the first major appearance of a technical term that is sufficiently important to also be defined in the Glossary near the back of *TYP* (pp. 225–233). If you read the Glossary definition of 'planet' now, you will find that it mentions 'Kuiper belt objects'. You have not met these yet, but you will soon, so don't worry about them for now. Generally speaking, if you come upon a term that you don't understand, look for it in the Glossary. If it is not there, the chances are that you can get by without being sure what it means. Sometimes though, I have explained a few non-glossary terms in this book, in the appropriate discussion section.

Activity 1.2

If you did this Activity, presumably you saw several dark blotches on the Moon's surface, which are visible even without optical aid. If you used binoculars or a telescope, you may have made out some mountain ranges that cast shadows, and possibly a few of the larger craters (craters will be described in Chapter 2); in fact, you should have obtained a rather better view than Galileo managed with his primitive telescope (Figure 1.3).

Activity 1.3

The visibility of the planets is continually changing. Sometimes there are no planets visible at certain times of the night. Therefore your chances of spotting a planet if you tried this Activity will have depended on when you did it.

Activity 3.1

I decided that in this paragraph the key parts were: the statement that we do not know which is true out of two options for the state of Mercury's core; the comment that the core is expected to have cooled down sufficiently to be solid; the contrary point that the magnetic field could indicate a liquid zone in the core; and the alternative option that today's magnetism could be 'frozen in' from the past. My highlighting is shown in Figure A3.

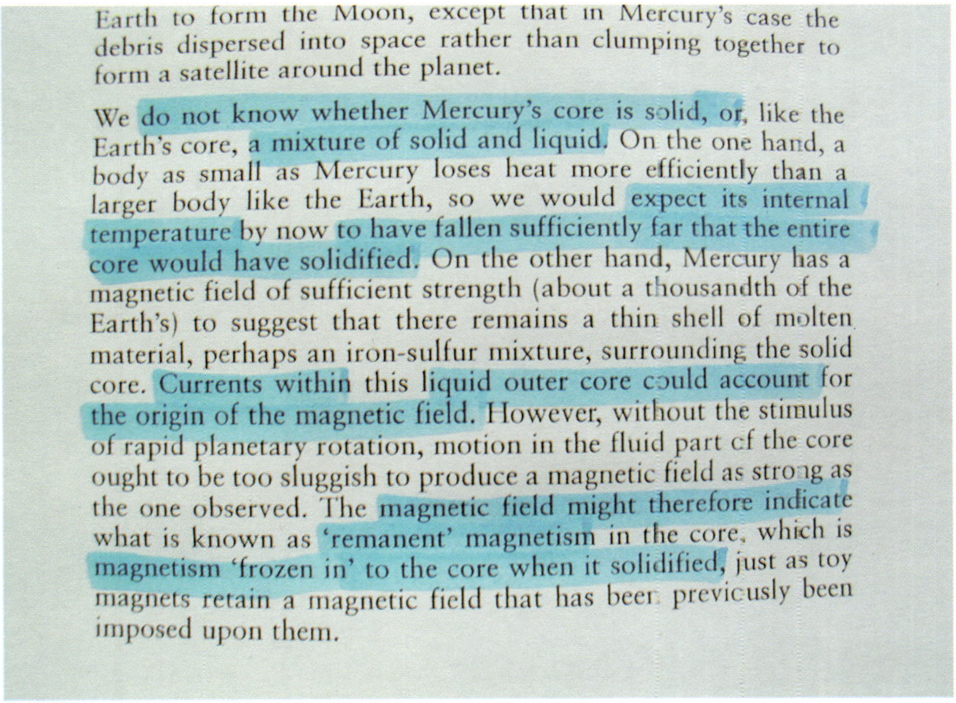

Earth to form the Moon, except that in Mercury's case the debris dispersed into space rather than clumping together to form a satellite around the planet.

We do not know whether Mercury's core is solid, or, like the Earth's core, a mixture of solid and liquid. On the one hand, a body as small as Mercury loses heat more efficiently than a larger body like the Earth, so we would expect its internal temperature by now to have fallen sufficiently far that the entire core would have solidified. On the other hand, Mercury has a magnetic field of sufficient strength (about a thousandth of the Earth's) to suggest that there remains a thin shell of molten material, perhaps an iron-sulfur mixture, surrounding the solid core. Currents within this liquid outer core could account for the origin of the magnetic field. However, without the stimulus of rapid planetary rotation, motion in the fluid part of the core ought to be too sluggish to produce a magnetic field as strong as the one observed. The magnetic field might therefore indicate what is known as 'remanent' magnetism in the core, which is magnetism 'frozen in' to the core when it solidified, just as toy magnets retain a magnetic field that has been previously been imposed upon them.

Figure A3 An example of highlighting key parts of the text on *TYP* p. 28.

Activity 3.2

You will have plenty of opportunity to explore the S196 CD-ROM during your study of this course, and I do not expect you to have mastered it yet. I hope you will use the 'Keyword Search' facility to help you to compare and contrast features and processes on different bodies. Be aware, however, that this facility is fairly primitive. For example, if you search for *crater* you will find twice as many examples as if you had searched for *impact crater*. Most of the extra examples will in fact be impact craters too, and do not appear in the *impact crater* search merely because neither their title nor caption happens to include the exact phrase *impact crater*. Similarly, a search for *craters* will yield fewer results than a search for *crater*, though a search for *crater* will find all the examples included in a search for *craters*.

When you complete the End of Course Assessment (ECA), you will need to use the 'Keyword Search' to call up some uncaptioned images that are the focus of some of the ECA questions.

Activity 4.1

This Activity is essentially a guided tour of part of the S196 CD-ROM. No additional discussion seems necessary.

Activity 5.1

No additional discussion.

Activity 15.1

(a) Asteroids are generally closer to the Sun, and QR_{322} is certainly not a main belt asteroid. 2001 QR_{322} could be a Centaur, which is a term introduced on *TYP* p. 98 for asteroids beyond Saturn. However, the orbit of QR_{322} lies some way beyond those of the known Centaurs, so perhaps it is best to regard it as a Kuiper belt object, while bearing in mind the statement in Chapter 8 that that there is probably no clear-cut distinction between asteroids and Kuiper belt objects. Certainly, at this distance from the Sun, we would expect 2001 QR_{322} to be an icy body.

(b) If it is a Trojan, it should occur very close to a point either 60° ahead of or 60° behind Neptune in its orbit (*TYP* p. 98).

(c) Neptune's orbital period is given (correctly) in the Chapter 12 *Planetary facts* table (*TYP* p. 184) as 163.7 years. Thus 'about 166 years' in the news item would appear to be an error for 'about 164 years'.

Acknowledgements

Grateful acknowledgement is made to the following sources for permission to reproduce material within this product. Please note that, except where noted below, planetary images used in Figures are courtesy of the National Aeronautics and Space Administration (NASA).

Figures

Figures 1.1 and 1.2: The Science Photo Library; *Figure 1.3 top*: from Van Helden, Siderius Nuncius or The Sidereal Messenger, pp. 44, 45 published by University of Chicago Press; *Figure 1.3 bottom*: NASA; *Figures 2.3–2.6*: James Garry – Fastlight; *Figure 5.2*: courtesy of Buck Sharpton, Lunar & Planetary Institute; *Figure 7.1 a, b, c*: All Rights Reserved Beagle 2; *Figure 7.3*: NASA/CXC/MPE/K. Dennerl *et al.*; *Figures 8.1 and 8.3*: NASA/Johns Hopkins University Applied Physics Laboratory; *Figure 8.4*: NASA and Southwest Research Institute; *Figures 9.1, 9.4, 10.1, 11.1*: Space Telescope Science Institute & NASA; *Figures 9.5 and 9.6*: University of Hawaii and Scott Sheppard/David Jewitt; *Figure 11.2*: Brett Gladman, University of British Columbia; *Figure 12.3*: Canada-France-Hawaii Telescope, C. Roddier, F. Roddier, J. E. Graves, M. Northcott and O. Guyon, Institute for Astronomy, Hawaii; *Figure 13.2*: David Jewitt, University of Hawaii; *Figure 14.1*: Al Schultz (CSC/STScI), Sally Heap (GSFC/NASA), and NASA; *Figure 14.2*: S. Korzennik, Harvard University, Smithsonian Centre for Astrophysics; *Figure 14.3*: NASA and A. Field (STScI); *Figure 14.4*: NASA and G. Bacon (STScI).

Every effort has been made to contact copyright holders. If any have been inadvertently overlooked the publishers will be pleased to make the necessary arrangements at the first opportunity.